White House Cookbook

Revised and Updated Centennial Edition

by Hugo Ziemann
(White House Steward under Grover Cleveland)
and F.L. Gillette

With healthy updates by
Patti Bazel Geil, R.D., and Tami Ross, R.D.

Houghton Mifflin Harcourt

BOSTON • NEW YORK

Copyright © 1996 by Patti Bazel Geil, R.D., and Tami Ross, R.D.
Published by Houghton Mifflin Harcourt Publishing Company
Published simultaneously in Canada
Previously published by Chronimed Publishing

For information and permission to reproduce selections from this book,
write to trade.permissions@hmhco.com or to Permissions, Houghton Mifflin
Harcourt Publishing Company, 3 Park Avenue, 19th Floor, New York, New York 10016.

www.hmhco.com

ISBN 0-471-34752-3

Printed in the United States of America

DOC 35 34 33 32 31 30 29 28 27 26 25
4500756324

ACKNOWLEDGMENTS

To Jack, who demonstrated many previously untapped political skills during the tasting, testing, and writing that went into this book. And to Kristen and Rachel, who may one day find themselves living in the White House!

—PBG

To my husband, Mike, who proved to be a great "diplomat" when sampling our creations. Your encouragement and support helped to make this cookbook a reality. And to precious baby Andrew, our "Commander-in-Chief," whose "inauguration" on June 3, 1995, made our humble home seem not so far from Pennsylvania Avenue.   —TAR

And to David Wexler, thanks for discovering this attic treasure and giving us the opportunity to make it our own!

Frances Folsom Cleveland

*T*ABLE OF *C*ONTENTS

★

NOTICE: CONSULT A HEALTH CARE PROFESSIONAL

The original recipes, household tips, and remedies from the 1894 edition of the *White House Cookbook* are provided here because of their historic significance and interest, and their publication in this updated edition is not an endorsement of them by the authors or publishers of this book. The original recipes and remedies contain ingredients which may not necessarily be healthful for some of today's lifestyles.

Readers are advised to seek the guidance of a licensed physician or healthcare professional before making any changes in a prescribed diet or healthcare regimen, as each individual case or need may vary. This book is intended for informational purposes only and is not for use as an alternative to appropriate medical care. While every effort has been made to ensure that the information is the most current available, new research findings, being released with increased frequency, may invalidate some data.

P R E F A C E

"Progress in civilization has been accompanied by progress in cookery."
—*Fannie Farmer*

Working on the centennial edition of the *White House Cookbook* and updating many of the book's original recipes has provided us with a view of the kitchen and the work of the homemaker of 100 years ago, as well as a good look at changes in the American diet over the past century.

In addition to the plethora of kitchen appliances and conveniences which make food preparation less time-consuming today than it was in the time of President and Mrs. Cleveland, the recipes of the 1890s suggest that present-day cooks enjoy a greater awareness of the elements of a proper diet. We are increasingly concerned about levels of fat, calories, and cholesterol, and about the amounts and varieties of nutrients in the dishes we serve and consume. Although proper nourishment was undoubtedly a goal for the authors of the 1894 edition of the book, the call for lard, fat, cream, eggs, or salt in most of the original recipes makes them unsuitable for today. Homemakers of that time spent the better part of their days at home in the kitchen, and there was a strong reliance on all manner of game, from wild hare to partridge.

While awareness of the importance of a proper diet has increased, precision has also entered the kitchen; today a recipe calls for "⅛ teaspoon of salt and ⅛ teaspoon of pepper," and not the "small quantity of salt and pepper" of 100 years ago. The precise measurements of today have also provided opportunity for technology to play a role in the monitoring of diets and in the planning of meals, menus, and cookbooks, allowing us to publish nutritional values and food exchanges, and to recommend recipes that incorporate substitutes to replace or reduce ingredients which contribute high levels of fat, cholesterol, and calories to a diet.

Although we have included some of the original recipes for historic interest only, we found more than enough material that could be updated with today's healthful diets in mind. The updated recipes we have included in this new centennial edition of the cookbook were selected with an eye toward meeting the health needs of today—low in fat, cholesterol, and sodium, yet high in convenience and good taste. Perhaps nothing dramatizes more the changes in the preparation of menus over the last century than the role that a computer now offers to meal planning; nutrient analyses of all the updated recipes has been performed, and food exchanges have also been provided with the aid of one more modern convenience that no one in the kitchen of the White House in 1894 could possibly have dreamed about.

Nutrient Analysis

Nutrient analysis of the updated recipes was performed using Nutritionist IV Diet Analysis Module, Version 4.0 (First DataBank, N-Squared Computing, The Hearst Corporation, 1111 Bayhill Drive, San Bruno, CA 94066).

Food Exchanges

Food exchanges are based on the amount of carbohydrate, protein, fat, and calories in foods. Each exchange has approximately the same amount of calories, carbohydrate, protein, and fat as another food on the same exchange list. The list allows persons monitoring their diets to know how to introduce variety in the diet when certain foods are required.

    Food exchange information in the *White House Cookbook* is based on the 1995 Exchange Lists for Meal Planning (The American Dietetic Association and The American Diabetes Association).

INTRODUCTION

★

The original 1894 edition of the *White House Cookbook* provides the reader with an eye-opening look at the food ways and culture of Americans 100 years ago. The book, with its recipes, menus, remedies, and household tips, offers an experience in American tradition. It is the purpose of this centennial edition of the work to preserve a bit of our rich heritage by making accessible recipes from the 1894 cookbook in both the original and in more practical and healthful, updated versions.

The background to the book is the White House of President Grover Cleveland—a period in American history which is perhaps better remembered by the events of the time than by any "Cleveland era." It was under Grover Cleveland, for example, that Labor Day became a legal holiday, but a hundred years later few of us know where appreciation for that piece of legislation should be directed. Also under President Cleveland, the Interstate Commerce Commission, the nation's first regulatory agency, was established, and the Departments of Labor and Agriculture were formed. Newspaper headlines of the time informed Americans that Hawaii had been declared a republic (with the help of the U.S. Marines); that a string of U.S. banks were going under because of the severe economic depression of the 1890s; that persons with annual incomes of more than $4,000 would begin to pay a two percent income tax; and that acetylsalicylic acid had been introduced under the trade name of aspirin. Overseas, Alfred Dreyfus was convicted of treason in a French military tribunal, the cinema had just been invented by Louis Lumiere, and China and Japan declared mutual war on each other.

Elsewhere, Robert Lewis Stevenson was publishing *Catriona,* Rudyard Kipling had completed *Barrack-Room Ballads,* the painters Cezanne, Toulouse-Lautrec, and Gaugin were at peaks in their careers, and Anton Dvorak was producing some of his best symphonies. At the White House, meanwhile, Hugo Ziemann, steward at the executive mansion, was compiling the *White House Cookbook* with Fannie L. Gillette, who in later years earned an entry in *Who Was Who in America* as a prominent cookbook author of the time.

From the perspective of 100 years, it seems that many more interesting culinary events were taking place outside of the White House than inside of it at the time the authors were writing. Coca-Cola was new on the market, having come out only a few short years before the publication of the *White House Cookbook;* shredded wheat was invented early in the second Cleveland administration; Aunt Jemima pancake mix was being promoted at a Chicago exposition; the beverage Postum had just been developed as a coffee substitute; and Milton Snavely Hershey was beginning to experiment with a new chocolate-making device. Within the White House, President Cleveland was probably not the gourmand that a prominent cookbook author would have hoped to have as his boss; the president's favorite dish was, purportedly, corned beef and cabbage. First Lady Frances Cleveland may have provided a source of cultural and gastronomic leadership at the White House, however. Though at 21, the youngest first lady in history, Frances Folsom Cleveland is said to have "excelled as a hostess." A dedication "To the wives of our presidents..." in an early edition of the *White House Cookbook* suggests a recognition by Ziemann of the role all the first ladies played in promoting and maintaining culinary standards at the White House and for the nation.

Technology, food trends, changing diets, and the language of the time might prevent many present-day readers of the original cookbook from wanting to find themselves in a kitchen of 1890 for any length of time—even the White House kitchen. Recipes were made from scratch in the late 19th century, and ingredients like cheese and butter were laboriously produced by hand. One cake recipe of the time called for 20 eggs as part of the batter, which the cook was instructed to beat vigorously for three hours! Also, 100 years ago, the endless bounty and variety of foods we know today did not exist. Until improved refrigeration, increased speed of transportation, and the industrialization of food processing took place, cooks were limited to the meats, fruits, and vegetables accessible in the area. Spices were used quite liberally in 19th century cooking, not only to preserve fresh foods, but to camouflage those that were not.

Even the clean, uncontaminated water we take for granted was not always available. Many Americans of the time died of waterborne diseases, including plague, cholera, and typhoid. Diseases of nutritional deficiency, such as scurvy, rickets, pellagra, beri-beri, and pernicious anemia were common. On the other hand, overindulgence in meat and starches abounded, as well-to-do Americans ate heavy diets adapted to the needs of pioneers, but not to their sedentary descendants. Almost all of the recipes in the original White House Cookbook contain at least one form of fat, butter, lard, suet, or cream. Obesity and gout were considered by many to be a mark of good living. Americans rarely bathed, rarely opened a window, and rarely took any regular exercise. In the mid-19th century, Sylvester Graham began to extol the virtues of bathing, exercise, and a whole wheat diet, but it was not until the early 1900s that the essential elements of healthful diets began to be understood.

During the past 100 years, there has been a shift in disease patterns. No longer are infectious diseases and vitamin deficiencies the predominant causes of death. An average lifespan has increased from approximately 50 years in 1900 to 75.8 years according to the most recently available statistics, so have the diseases of dietary excess, including obesity, diabetes mellitus, and cardiovascular disease. Chronic diseases such as these, as well as some forms of cancer, are currently among the leading causes of death in the United States that are related to diet. The foremost health authorities now recommend we reduce our consumption of fat, saturated fat, and cholesterol; achieve and maintain a desirable body weight; reduce our intake of sodium; and increase the amount of complex carbohydrates and fiber in our diet.

The authenticity of the original recipes selected for this centennial edition has been maintained, along with the language of the period, revealing changes that have occurred in the language as well as in the culinary arts. There has been no attempt to update archaic expressions, such as "scrag" (the lean end of the neck of veal or mutton), to modernize spellings (lima bean was formerly capitalized, reflecting more closely the origin of the word), or to clarify cooking instructions ("an oven hot enough to brown a teaspoonful of flour in 5 minutes," is an example of the imprecision of the time); nor has there been an attempt to break up the long paragraphs that were the style 100 years ago. An exception is the occasional modification of punctuation when it has been added or corrected to facilitate reading.

The *White House Cookbook* is a small treasure of Americana. The book's rules of etiquette inform us about the customs of the day—"Never ask to be helped to soup a second time"; the household tips reveal the life of the homemaker of the 1890s; and from the recipes we learn about the diet and the language of Americans 100 years ago. This updated centennial edition of the *White House Cookbook* offers a wonderful opportunity to experience a slice of life in the 19th century and to enjoy updated, classic American recipes such as those from Barbara Bush and Hillary Rodham Clinton, our two most recent First Ladies. While we enjoyed their original recipes, we were able to find ways to lighten and update them without losing their good taste.

★

WHITE HOUSE COOKBOOK

★

Hillary Rodham Clinton's Original

CHOCOLATE CHIP COOKIES

1 1/2 cups unsifted all-purpose flour

1 teaspoon salt

1 teaspoon baking soda

1 cup solid vegetable shortening

1 cup firmly packed light brown sugar

1/2 cup granulated sugar

1 teaspoon vanilla

2 eggs

2 cups old-fashioned rolled oats

12-ounce package semi-sweet chocolate chips

Preheat oven to 350°. Grease baking sheets. Combine flour, salt, and baking soda. In a separate bowl, beat together shortening, sugars, and vanilla until creamy. Add eggs, beating until light and fluffy. Gradually beat in flour mixture and rolled oats. Stir in chocolate chips. Drop batter by well-rounded teaspoonsful onto greased baking sheets. Bake 8-10 minutes or until golden. Cool cookies on sheets on wire rack for 2 minutes. Remove cookies to wire rack to cool completely.

Preparation time: 20 minutes
Baking time: 8-10 minutes per pan

NUTRITION INFORMATION

Servings per recipe: 54—Serving size: 1 cookie

Protein 1 g, Carbohydrate 15 g, Fat 6 g, Saturated Fat 1 g,
Cholesterol 4 mg, Sodium 66 mg, Dietary Fiber <1 g

Calories 118
From protein: 3%; From carbohydrate: 51%; From fat: 46%

Food Exchanges: 1 starch, 1 fat

Lower-Fat Version

CHOCOLATE CHIP COOKIES

1 1/2 cups unsifted all-purpose flour

1/2 teaspoon salt

1 teaspoon baking soda

2/3 cup reduced-fat stick margarine

1 cup firmly packed light brown sugar

1/2 cup granulated sugar

1 teaspoon vanilla

1 teaspoon butter flavoring

1/2 cup egg substitute

2 cups old-fashioned rolled oats

10 ounces mini chocolate chips

Cooking spray

Preheat oven to 350°. Combine flour, salt, and baking soda in one bowl. In a separate bowl, beat together margarine, sugars, vanilla, and butter flavoring until creamy. Add egg substitute, beating until light and fluffy. Gradually beat in flour mixture and rolled oats. Stir in chocolate chips. Drop batter by well-rounded teaspoonsful onto baking sheets coated with cooking spray. Bake 8-10 minutes or until golden. Cool cookies on sheets on wire rack for 2 minutes. Remove cookies to wire rack to cool completely.

Preparation time: 20 minutes
Baking time: 8 10 minutes per pan

NUTRITION INFORMATION

Servings per recipe: 54—Serving size: 1 cookie

Protein 1 g, Carbohydrate 14 g, Fat 3 g, Saturated Fat <1 g,
Cholesterol <1 mg, Sodium 75 mg, Dietary Fiber <1 g

Calories 87
From protein: 5%; From carbohydrate: 64%; From fat: 31%

Food Exchanges: 1 starch

Barbara Bush's Original

⊁SCOTCH⊁ SHORTBREAD

2 cups sifted all-purpose flour

1/4 teaspoon baking powder

1/4 teaspoon salt

1 cup butter

3/4 cup sifted powdered sugar

2 tablespoons granulated sugar

Sift flour with baking powder and salt. In a separate bowl, cream butter and powdered sugar until light and fluffy. Gradually mix in flour; mix well. Refrigerate dough until chilled, about 45 minutes. Press dough into ungreased 8"x 8"x 2" baking pan. Prick top of dough with fork. Sprinkle with granulated sugar. Bake at 350° for 35-40 minutes or until top is lightly browned. Cut into 16 squares while warm.

Preparation time: 10 minutes

Chilling time: 45 minutes

Baking time: 35-40 minutes

NUTRITION INFORMATION

Servings per recipe: 16—Serving size: 1 bar

Protein 2 g, Carbohydrate 18 g, Fat 12 g, Saturated Fat 7 g, Cholesterol 31 mg, Sodium 159 mg, Dietary Fiber <1 g

Calories 188

From protein: 4%; From carbohydrate: 38%; From fat: 57%

Food Exchanges: 1 starch, 2 fat

Lower-Fat Version

❄SCOTCH❄ SHORTBREAD

2 cups sifted all-purpose flour

1/4 teaspoon baking powder

1/8 teaspoon salt

3/4 cup reduced-fat stick margarine

3/4 cup sifted powdered sugar

1 tablespoon light corn syrup

Cooking spray

2 tablespoons granulated sugar

Sift flour with baking powder and salt. In a separate bowl, cream margarine and powdered sugar until light and fluffy. Beat in corn syrup. Gradually mix in flour; mix well. Refrigerate dough until chilled, about 45 minutes. Press dough into ungreased 8"x 8"x 2" baking pan coated with cooking spray. Prick top of dough with fork. Sprinkle with granulated sugar. Bake at 350° for 35-40 minutes or until top is lightly browned. Cut into 16 squares while warm.

Preparation time: 10 minutes
Chilling time: 45 minutes
Baking time: 35-40 minutes

NUTRITION INFORMATION

Servings per recipe: 16—Serving size: 1 bar

Protein 2 g, Carbohydrate 19 g, Fat 4 g, Saturated Fat 1 g,
Cholesterol 0, Sodium 124 mg, Dietary Fiber <1 g

Calories 120
From protein: 7%; From carbohydrate: 63%; From fat: 30%

Food Exchanges: 1 starch, 1 fat

State Dining Room.

Excerpted from the original
WHITE HOUSE COOKBOOK
1894

Small Points on Table Etiquette.

Delicacy of manner at table stamps both man and woman, for one can, at a glance, discern whether a person has been trained to eat well—i.e. to hold the knife and fork properly, to eat without the slightest sound of the lips, to drink quietly, to use the napkin rightly, to make no noise with any of the implements of the table, and last, but not least, to eat slowly and masticate the food thoroughly. All these points should be most carefully taught to children, and then they will always feel at their ease at the grandest tables in the land. There is no position where the innate refinement of a person is more fully exhibited than at the table, and nowhere that those who have not been trained in table etiquette feel more keenly their deficiencies. The knife should never be used to carry food to the mouth, but only to cut it up into small mouthfuls; then place it upon the plate at one side, and take the fork in the right hand, and eat all the food with it. When both have been used finally, they should be laid diagonally across the plate, with both handles toward the right hand; this is understood by well-trained waiters to be the signal for removing them, together with the plate.

Be careful to keep the mouth shut closely while masticating the food. It is the opening of the lips which causes the smacking which seems very disgusting. Chew your food well, but do it silently, and be careful to take small mouthfuls. The knife can be used to cut the meat finely, as large pieces of meat are not healthful, and appear very indelicate. At many tables, two, three or more knives and forks are placed on the table, the knives at the right hand of the plate, the forks at the left,—knife and fork for each course, so that there need be no replacing of them after the breakfast and dinner is served. The smaller ones, which are for game, dessert, or for hot cakes at breakfast, can be tucked under the edges of the plate, and the large ones, for the meat and vegetables, are placed outside of them. Be very careful not to clatter your knifes and forks upon your plates, but use them without noise. When passing the plate for a second helping, lay them together at one side of the plate, with handles to the right. When you are helped to anything, do not wait until the rest of the company are provided, as it is not considered good breeding. Soup is always served for the first course, and it should be eaten with dessert spoons, and taken from the sides, not the tips, of them, without any sound of the lips, and not sucked into the mouth audibly from the ends of the spoon. Bread should not be broken into soup or gravy. Never ask to be helped to soup a second time. The hostess may ask you to take a second plate, but you will politely decline. Fish chowder, which is served in soup plates, is said to be an exception which proves this rule, and when eating of that, it is correct to take a second plateful if desired.

Another generally neglected obligation is that of spreading butter on one's bread as it lies in one's plate, or but slightly lifted at one end of the plate; it is very frequently buttered in the air, bitten in gouges, and still held in the face and eyes of the table with the marks of the teeth on it. This is certainly not altogether pleasant, and it is better to cut it, a bit at a time, after buttering it, and put piece by piece in the mouth with one's finger and thumb. Never help yourself to butter, or any other food with your own knife or fork. It is not considered good taste to mix food on the same plate. Salt must be left on the side of the plate and never on the tablecloth.

Let us mention a few things concerning the eating of which there is sometimes doubt. A cream-cake and anything of similar nature would be eaten with knife and fork, never bitten. Asparagus—which should be always served on bread or toast so as to absorb superfluous moisture—may be taken from the finger and thumb; if it is fit to be set before you, the whole of it may be eaten. Pastry should be broken and eaten with a fork, never cut with a knife. Raw oysters should be eaten with a fork, also fish. Peas and beans, as well known, require the fork only; however food that cannot be held with a fork should be eaten with a spoon. Potatoes, if mashed, should be mashed with the fork. Green corn should be eaten from the cob; but it must be held with a single hand.

Celery, cresses, olives, radishes, and relishes of that kind are, of course, to be eaten with the fingers; the salt should be laid upon one's plate, not upon the cloth. Fish is to be eaten with the fork, without the assistance of the knife; a bit of bread in the left hand sometimes helps one to master a refactory morsel. Fresh fruit should be eaten with a silver-bladed knife, especially pears, apples, etc.

Berries, of course, are to be eaten with a spoon. In England they are served with their hulls on, and three or four are considered an ample quantity. But then in England they are many times the size of ours; there they take the big berry by the stem, dip into powdered sugar, and eat it as we do the turnip radish. It is not proper to drink with a spoon in the cup; nor should one, by-the-way, ever quite drain a cup or glass.

Don't, when you drink, elevate your glass as if you were going to stand it inverted on your nose. Bring the glass perpendicularly to the lips, and then lift it to a slight angle. Do this easily.

Drink sparingly while eating. It is far better for the digestion not to drink tea or coffee until the meal is finished. Drink gently, and not pour it down your throat like water turned out of a pitcher.

When seating yourself at the table, unfold your napkin and lay it across your lap in such a manner that it will not slide off upon the floor; a gentleman should place it across his right knee. Do not tuck it into your neck like a child's bib. For an old person, however, it is well to attach the napkin to a napkin hook and slip it into the vest or dress buttonholes, to protect their garments, or sew a broad tape at two places on the napkin, and pass it over the head. When the soup is eaten, wipe the mouth carefully with the napkin, and use it to wipe the hands after meals. Finger bowls are not a general institution, and yet they seem to be quite as needful as the napkin, for the fingers are also liable to become a little soiled in eating. They can be had quite cheaply, and should be half-filled with water, and placed upon the side table or butler's tray, with the dessert, bread and cheese, etc. They are passed to each person half filled with water, placed on a parti-colored napkin with a dessert plate underneath, when the dessert is placed upon the table. A leaf or two of sweet verbena, an orange flower, or a small slice of lemon, is usually put into each bowl to rub upon the fingers. The slice of lemon is most commonly used. The finger tips are slightly dipped into the bowl, the lemon juice is squeezed upon them, and then they are dried softly upon the napkin. At dinner parties and luncheons they are indispensable.

Spoons are sometimes used with firm puddings, but forks are the better style. A spoon should never be turned over in the mouth.

Ladies have frequently an affected way of holding the knife half-way down its length, as if it were too big for their little hands; but this is as awkward a way as it is weak; the knife should be grasped freely by the handle only, the fore-finger being the only one to touch the blade, and that only along the back of the blade at its root, and no further down.

At the conclusion of a course, where they have been used, knife and fork should be laid side by side across the middle of the plate—never crossed; the old custom of crossing them was in obedience to an ancient religious formula. The servant should offer everything at the left of the guest, that the guest may be at liberty to use the right hand. If one has been given a napkin ring, it is necessary to fold one's napkin and use the ring; otherwise the napkin should be left unfolded. One's teeth are not to be picked at table; but if it is impossible to hinder it, it should be done behind the napkin. One may pick a bone at the table, but, as with corn, only one hand is allowed to touch it; yet one can easily get enough from it with knife and fork, which is certainly the more elegant way of doing; and to take her teeth to it gives a lady the look of caring a little too much for the pleasures of the table; one is, however, on no account to suck one's finger after it.

Whenever there is any doubt as to the best way to do a thing, it is wise to follow that which is the most rational, and that will almost invariably be found to be proper etiquette. To be at ease is a great step towards enjoying your own dinner, and making yourself agreeable to the company. There is reason for everything in polite usage; thus the reason why one does not blow a thing to cool it, it is not only that it is an inelegant and vulgar action intrinsically, but because it may be offensive to others—cannot help being so, indeed; and it, moreover implies, haste, which, whether from greediness or a desire to get away, is equally objectionable. Everything else may be as easily traced to its origin in the fit and becoming.

If, to conclude, one seats one's self properly at table and takes reason into account, one will do tolerably well. One must not pull one's chair too closely to the table, for the natural result of that is the inability to use one's knife and fork without inconveniencing one's neighbor; the elbows are to be held well in and close to one's side, which cannot be done if the chair is too near the board. One must not lie or lean along the table, nor rest one's arms upon it. Nor is one to touch any of the dishes; if a member of the family, one can exercise all the duties of hospitality through servants, and wherever there are servants, neither family nor guests are to pass or help from any dish. Finally, when rising from your chair, leave it where it stands.

State Dinner at White House

Blue Points.   Haute Sauterne.
Amontillado.

POTAGES.

Potage tortue à l'Anglaise Consommé Printanière Royale.

HORS D'OEUVRES.

Canape à la Russe.   Timbales à la Talleyrand.
Rauenthaler Berg.

POISSONS.

Saumon, Sauce Hollandaise.   Grenadines de Bass.
Pommes de Terre Duchesse.   Cucumber Salade.
Ernest Jeroy.

RELEVÉS.

Sele d'Agneau, Sauce Menthe.
Filet de Boeuf à la Richelieu.
Chateau Margause.

ENTRÉES.

Ris de Veau à la Perigneux.
Cotellettes d'Agneau d'or Maison.
Terrapin à la Maryland.

Punch Cardinal.
Clas de Vougeot.

RÔTI.

Canvas Back Duck.

ENTREMETS.

German Asparagus.   Petit Pois.
Gelée au Champagne.   Plombiere aux Framboise.

Pudding Diplomate.
Café.   Liqueurs.
Fruits.   Fromage.

Excerpted from the original

WHITE HOUSE COOKBOOK
1894

*D*inner Giving

The laying of the table and the treatment of guests.

In giving "dinners," the apparently trifling details are of great importance when taken as a whole.

We gather around our board agreeable persons, and they pay us and our dinner the courtesy of dressing for the occasion, and this reunion should be a time of profit as well as pleasure. There are certain established laws by which "dinner giving" is regulated in polite society; and it may not be amiss to give a few observances in relation to them. One of the first is that an invited guest should arrive at the house of his host at least a quarter of an hour before the time appointed for dinner. In laying the table for dinner all the linen should be a spotless white throughout, and underneath the linen tablecloth should be spread one of thick cotton-flannel or baize, which gives the linen a heavier and finer appearance, also deadening the sound of moving dishes. Large and neatly folded napkins (ironed without starch), with pieces of bread three or four inches long, placed between the folds, but not to completely conceal it, are laid on each plate. An ornamental centre-piece, or a vase filled with a few rare flowers, is put on the centre of the table, in place of the large table castor, which has gone into disuse, and is rarely seen now on well-appointed tables. A few choice flowers make a charming variety in the appearance of even the most simply laid table, and a pleasing variety at table is quite as essential to the enjoyment of the repast as is a good choice of dishes, for the eye in fact should be gratified as much as the palate.

All dishes should be arranged in harmony with the decorations of the flowers, such as covers, relishes, confectionery, and small sweets. Garnishing of dishes has also a great deal to do with the appearance of a dinner-table, each dish garnished sufficiently to be in good taste without looking absurd.

Beside each plate should be laid as many knives, forks, and spoons as will be required for the several courses, unless the hostess prefers to have them brought on with each change. A glass of water, and when wine is served glasses for it, and individual salt-cellars may be placed at every plate. Water-bottles are now much in vogue with corresponding tumblers to cover them; these, accompanied with dishes of broken ice, may be arranged in suitable places. When butter is served, a special knife is used, and that, with all other required service, may be left to the judgment and taste of the hostess, in the proper placing of the various aids to her guests' comfort.

The dessert plates should be set ready, each with a doily and a finger-glass partly filled with water, in which is dropped a slice of lemon; these with extra knives, forks, and spoons, should be on the side-board ready to be placed beside the guest between the courses when required.

If preferred, the "dinner" may all be served from the side-table, thus relieving the host from the task of carving. A plate is set before each guest, and the dish carved is presented by the waiter on the left-hand side of each guest. At the end of each course the plates give way for those of the next. If not served from the side-table, the dishes are brought in ready carved, and placed before the host and hostess, then served and placed upon the waiter's salver, to be laid by that attendant before the guest.

Soup and fish being the first course, plates of soup are usually placed on the table before the dinner is announced; or if the hostess wishes the soup served at the table, the soup-tureen, containing hot soup, and warm soup-plates are placed before the seat of the hostess. Soup and fish being disposed of, then come the joints or roasts, entrees (made dishes), poultry, etc., also relishes.

After dishes have been passed that are required no more, such as vege-tables, hot sauces, etc., the dishes containing them may be set upon the side-board, ready to be taken away.

Jellies and sauces, when not to be eaten as a dessert, should be helped on the dinner-plate, not on a small side dish as was the former usage.

If a dish be on the table, some parts of which are preferred to others, according to the taste of the individuals, all should have the opportunity of choice. The host will simply ask each one if he has any preference for a particular part; if he replies in the negative, you are not to repeat the question, nor insist that he must have a preference.

Do not attempt to eulogize your dishes, or apologize that you cannot recommend them—this is extreme bad taste; as also is the vaunting of the excellence of your wines, etc., etc.

Do not insist upon your guests partaking of particular dishes. Do not ask persons more than once, and never force a supply upon their plates. It is ill-bred, though common, to press any one to eat; and, moreover, it is a great annoyance to many.

In winter, plates should always be warmed, but not made hot. Two kinds of animal food, or two kinds of dessert, should not be eaten off of one plate, and there should never be more than two kinds of vegetables with one course. Asparagus, green corn, cauliflower and raw tomatoes comprise one course in place of a salad. All meats should be cut across the grain in very thin slices. Fish, at dinner, should be baked or boiled, never fried or broiled. Baked ham may be used in every course after fish, sliced thin and handed after the regular course is disposed of.

The hostess should retain her plate, knife and fork, until her guests have finished.

The crumb-brush is not used until the preparation for bringing in the dessert; then all the glasses are removed, except the flowers, the water-tumblers, and the glass of wine which the guest wishes to retain with his dessert. The dessert plate containing the finger-bowl, also a dessert knife and fork, should then be set before each guest, who at once removes the finger-bowl and its doily, and the knife and fork to the table, leaving the plate ready to be used for any dessert chosen.

Finely sifted sugar should always be placed upon the table to be used with puddings, pies, fruit, etc., and if cream is required, let it stand by the dish it is to be served with.

To lay a dessert for a small entertainment and a few guests outside of the family, it may consist simply of two dishes of fresh fruit in season, two of dried fruits and two each of cakes and nuts.

Coffee and tea are served lastly, poured into tiny cups and served clear, passed around on a tray to each guest, then the sugar and cream passed that each person may be allowed to season his black coffee or café noir to suit himself.

A family dinner, even with a few friends, can be made quite attractive and satisfactory without much display or expense; consisting first of good soup, then fish garnished with suitable additions, followed by a roast, then vegetables and some made dishes, a salad, crackers, cheese and olives, then dessert. This sensible meal, well cooked and neatly served, is pleasing to almost any one, and is within the means of any housekeeper in ordinary circumstances.

*M*anagement and Direction of Dinners and Receptions on State Occasions at the White House

Etiquette as observed in European courts is not known at the White House.

The President's Secretary issues invitations by direction of the President to the distinguished guests.

The Usher in charge of the cloak-room hands to the gentleman on arrival an envelope containing a diagram of the table, whereon the name and seat of the respective guest and the lady he is to escort to dinner are marked.

A card corresponding with his name is placed on the napkin belonging to the cover of the seat he will occupy.

The President's seat is in the middle of the table. The most distinguished guests sit on his right and left. If their wives are present they will occupy these seats, and the gentlemen will be seated next to the President's wife whose seat is directly opposite the President.

Official dinners all over the world are always served after the French fashion, and are divided into three distinct parts. Two of them are served from the kitchen, and the third from the pantry.

The first part of the dinner served French-style includes from oysters on the shell to the sherbets.

The second service continues to the sweet dishes.

The third includes ice, cakes, fruits, cheeses, which are all understood as desserts, and are dressed in the pantry.

All principal dishes which are artistically decorated are shown to the President first, then are carried around the table before being carved by the Steward in the pantry.

Fancy folding of the napkins is considered out of fashion; plain square folded, so as to show monogram in the middle, is much preferred.

The following diagram will illustrate the arrangement of the glasses on the table.

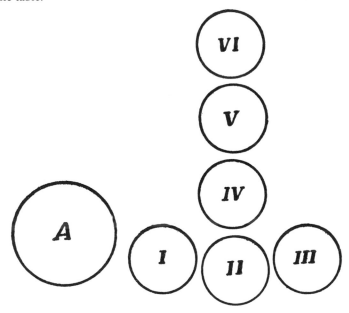

DIAGRAM ILLUSTRATING HOW TO ARRANGE GLASSES ON TABLE.

	I—Glass for Sauterne.	IV—Glass for Water.
A—Plate.	II—Glass for Sherry.	V—Glass for Champagne.
	III—Glass for Rhine Wine.	VI—Glass for Burgundy.

Flower decorations on the table are to be in flat designs, so as not to obscure the view of the guests.

Corsage boquets for ladies consist of not more than eight large roses tied together by silk ribbon, with the name of the lady stamped on in gold letters.

Gentlemen's bouttonieres consist only of one rosebud.

Boquets for ladies are to be placed on the right side; for gentlemen, on the napkin next to card bearing his name.

Printed menus are never used on any official occasion.

The private dinners menus are either printed or written on a plain card and placed on each cover.

Liquors, cordials, cigars are served on a separate table after the ladies have retired to the parlor.

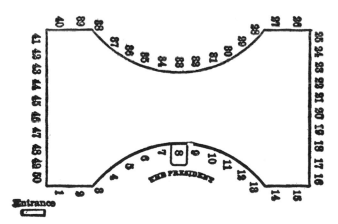

Mrs. Cleveland's Wedding Lunch.
JUNE 4TH, '86

Consommé en tasse.

Soft Shell Crabs.   *Chateau Iquem.*

Coquilles de Ris de Veau.

Snipes on Toast.
Lettuce and Tomato Salade.
Moet & Chandon.

Fancy Ice-cream.
Cakes.
Tea.   *Coffee.*
Fruits.   *Mottos.*

General Grant's Birthday Dinner.

Clams   Haute Sauterne.

POTAGES.

Consommé Impèratrice Bisque de Crabes.
Amontillado.

HORS D'OEUVRE VARIES.

Bouchées à la Règènce.

POISSON.

Truites de rivière Hollandaise vert pré.
Pommes de terre à la Parisienne.
Coucombres.   Johannisberger.

RELEVÉ.

Filet de Boeuf à la Bernardi
Ernest Jeroy.

ENTRÉES.

Ailes de Poulets à la Perigord.   Petits Pois au Beune.
Caisses de ris de Veau à l'Italienne.   Haricots verts.
Aspèrges, sauce Crème

SORBET FANTAISIE.

RÔTI.

Squabs.
Salade de Laitue.   Nuits.

ENTREMETS SUCRÉS.

Crout aux Mille Fruits.   Cornets à la Chantilly.
Gelée à la Prunelle.

PIECES MONTÉES.

Glace Varietées.
Fruits.   Petits Fours.   Café.

Buffet for 1,000 People.
Cold Service.

Consommé en tasse.

Sandwiches.   Caviar on Toast.
Radishes.   Celery.
Cold Salmon Mayonnaise.
Lobster and Shrimp Salad.

Westphalia Ham à la gelée.

Cold Game in Season.
Boned Turkey.   Galautine of Faison.

Mayonnaise of Chicken.   Cold Turkey.
Fillet of Beef.   Game Pie.

Saddle of Venison, Currant Jelly.
Russian Salad.

Neapolitaine Ice-cream.   Water Ices.
Nesselrode Puddings.

Claret and Champagne Jellies.

Biscuits Glacée.   Charlotte Glacée.
Assorted Cakes.   Assorted Candies.

Tea.   Coffee.   Lemonade.

BEVERAGES

⚜ Kahlúa Cocoa ⚜

A tasty treat for a cozy night by the fire.

1/3 cup fat-free chocolate syrup
1/4 cup boiling water
4 cups skim milk
1/4 cup Kahlúa®

Combine chocolate syrup and water in medium saucepan. Add milk and stir until blended. Place pan over medium heat until cocoa is hot, but not boiling. Stir in Kahlúa. May garnish with miniature marshmallows or light whipped topping.

Preparation time: 15 minutes

N U T R I E N T   I N F O R M A T I O N

Servings per recipe: 5—Serving size: 1 cup

Protein 7 g, Carbohydrate 29 g, Fat 1 g, Saturated Fat <1 g, Cholesterol 3 mg, Sodium 133 mg, Dietary Fiber 0

Calories 174
From protein: 16%; From carbohydrate: 67%;
From fat: 5%; From alcohol: 12%

Food Exchanges: 1 skim milk, 1 fruit

C O C O A

from the White House Cookbook, 1894

Six tablespoonfuls of cocoa to each pint of water, as much milk as water, sugar to taste. Rub cocoa smooth in a little cold water; have ready on the fire a pint of boiling water; stir in grated cocoa paste. Boil twenty minutes, add milk and boil five minutes more, stirring often. Sweeten in cups so as to suit different tastes.

FOR A SUMMER DRAUGHT

from the White House Cookbook, 1894

The juice of one lemon, a tumblerful of cold water, pounded
sugar to taste, half a small teaspoonful of carbonate of soda.
Squeeze the juice from the lemon; strain and add it to the water,
with sufficient pounded sugar to sweeten the whole nicely.
When well mixed, put in the soda, stir well and drink
while the mixture is in an effervescing state.

❄A SUMMER BREEZE❄

A great thirst quencher to beat the summer heat!

1/2 cup sugar

4 cups unsweetened apple juice

1 cup freshly squeezed lemon juice

1 cup apricot nectar

1 cup chilled club soda

14 maraschino cherries

Combine sugar, juices, and nectar in 2-quart pan. Stir over medium heat until sugar is dissolved. Remove from heat. Pour into pitcher and chill. When ready to serve, stir in club soda and float cherries on top. Pour into glasses over crushed ice.

If a slushy beverage is desired, pour the juice combination into freezer bags and freeze. Thaw until slushy before serving. If pressed for time, beverage may be thawed in microwave. Place in pitcher or punch bowl. Stir in club soda and float cherries on top.

Preparation time: 50 minutes (including chilling time)
Freezing time (if desired): 3 hours
Thawing time: 30 minutes

NUTRIENT INFORMATION

Servings per recipe: 7—Serving size: 1 cup

Protein <1 g, Carbohydrate 45 g, Fat <1 g, Saturated Fat <1 g, Cholesterol 0, Sodium 30 mg, Dietary Fiber <1 g

Calories 188
From protein: 1%; From carbohydrate: 96%; From fat: 3%

Food Exchanges: 3 fruit

⊁Egg Nog⊱ With Orange and Nutmeg

A holiday treat you can enjoy without guilt!

3/4 cup liquid egg substitute

6 cups skim milk, divided

1/2 cup sugar

1/8 teaspoon salt

1/2 teaspoon grated orange rind

1 teaspoon vanilla extract

1 1/2 teaspoons rum extract

Ground nutmeg for garnish

*P*lace egg substitute, 5 cups milk, sugar, salt, and orange rind in a large pan. Stir constantly over medium heat until thickened. Remove from heat and stir in extracts. Cover and chill 3 hours. Before serving, mix in remaining cup of milk and sprinkle with nutmeg.

Preparation time: 20 minutes
Chilling time: 3 hours

N U T R I E N T   I N F O R M A T I O N

Servings per recipe: 7—Serving size: 1 cup

*Protein 10 g, Carbohydrate 25 g, Fat 1 g, Saturated Fat <1 g,
Cholesterol 4 mg, Sodium 194 mg, Dietary Fiber 0*

Calories 149
From protein: 27%; From carbohydrate: 67%; From fat: 6%

Food Exchanges: 1 starch, 1 skim milk

EGG NOG

from the White House Cookbook, 1894

Beat the yolks of twelve eggs very light, stir in as much white sugar as they will dissolve, pour in gradually one glass of brandy to cook the egg, one glass of old whisky, one grated nutmeg, and three pints of rich milk. Beat the whites to a froth and stir in last.

TO MAKE HOT PUNCH

from the White House Cookbook, 1894

Half a pint of rum, half a pint of brandy, quarter of a pound of sugar, one large lemon, half a teaspoonful of nutmeg, one pint of boiling water.

Rub the sugar over the lemon until it has absorbed all the yellow part of the skin, then put the sugar into a punch bowl; add the lemon juice (free from pips) and mix these two ingredients, well together. Pour over them the boiling water, stir well together, add the rum, brandy and nutmeg; mix thoroughly and the punch will be ready to serve. It is very important in making good punch that all the ingredients are thoroughly incorporated; and to insure success, the processes of mixing must be diligently attended to.
(This is an old-style punch.)

⭐SIMPLY⭐ CINNAMON CIDER

A family favorite for pumpkin-carving or tree-trimming parties.

3 quarts apple cider
5 cups ginger ale
1 1/2 cups red cinnamon candy
6 cinnamon sticks
6 whole cloves

*C*ombine cider and ginger ale in stock pot. Place candy and spices in a spice basket or cheesecloth bag and immerse in cider. Cover pot and simmer for 45 minutes. Remove spices before serving.

Just as tasty reheated the next day!

Preparation time: 10 minutes
Cooking time: 45 minutes

Nutrient Information

Servings per recipe: 17—Serving size: 1 cup

*Protein <1 g, Carbohydrate 40 g, Fat <1 g, Saturated Fat <1 g,
Cholesterol 0, Sodium 13 mg, Dietary Fiber <1 g*

Calories 167
From protein: 1%; From carbohydrate: 96%; From fat: 3%

Food Exchanges: 3 fruit

⁂ SPARKLING ⁂ STRAWBERRY SPRITZER

May be served as a refreshing punch or as a pleasing low-calorie snack.

2 (20-ounce) packages frozen unsweetened strawberries, thawed
48 ounces chilled white grape juice
1-liter chilled club soda

*P*lace strawberries in an electric blender and process until smooth. Pour strawberry purée into punch bowl or pitcher and stir in juice, then club soda. Serve immediately.

Garnish with fresh strawberries and mint leaves.

Preparation time: 15 minutes

NUTRIENT INFORMATION

Servings per recipe: 14—Serving size: 1 cup

Protein 1 g, Carbohydrate 22 g, Fat <1 g, Saturated Fat <1 g, Cholesterol 0, Sodium 19 mg, Dietary Fiber 1 g

Calories 97
From protein: 4%; From carbohydrate: 88%; From fat: 5%

Food Exchanges: 2 fruit

STRAWBERRY WATER

from the White House Cookbook, 1894

*T*ake one cupful of ripe hulled berries; crush with a
wooden spoon, mixing with the mass a quarter of a
pound of pulverized sugar and half a pint of cold water. Pour the
mixture into a fine sieve, rub through and filter till clear; add the
strained juice of one lemon and one and a half pints of cold water,
mix thoroughly and set in ice chest till wanted.

This makes a nice, cool drink on a warm day and
easily to be made in strawberry season.

PINEAPPLE ADE

from the White House Cookbook, 1894

*P*are and slice some very ripe pineapples; then cut the slices into small pieces. Put them with all their juice into a large pitcher, and sprinkle among them plenty of powdered white sugar. Pour on boiling water, allowing a small half pint to each pineapple. Cover the pitcher and let it stand till quite cool, occasionally pressing down the pineapple with a spoon. Then set the pitcher for a while in ice. Lastly, strain the infusion into another vessel and transfer it to tumblers, putting into each glass some more sugar and a bit of ice. This beverage will be found delicious.

❧ PERFECT PINEAPPLE ❧ PUNCH

A delicious "not-too-sweet" treat at receptions and showers.

3 quarts unsweetened pineapple juice

1 cup sugar

2 tablespoons almond extract

1 2-liter ginger ale

In a large container, mix all ingredients then pour punch into freezer bags. Freeze. Thaw until slushy before serving. If pressed for time, punch may be thawed in microwave. Place into punch bowl and pour ginger ale over. Stir and serve.

This recipe can easily be doubled.

Preparation time: 10 minutes
Freezing time: 3 hours
Thawing time: 30 minutes

NUTRIENT INFORMATION

Servings per recipe: 20—Serving size: 1 cup

Protein <1 g, Carbohydrate 40 g, Fat <1 g, Saturated Fat <1 g, Cholesterol 0, Sodium 9 mg, Dietary Fiber <1 g

Calories 167
From protein: 1%; From carbohydrate: 96%; From fat: 3%

Food Exchanges: 3 fruit

"Tranquility is the old man's milk."

—*Thomas Jefferson, June 24, 1797*

Excerpted from the original
WHITE HOUSE COOKBOOK
1894

The Healing Properties of Tea and Coffee.

The medical properties of these two beverages are considerable. Tea is used advantageously in inflammatory diseases and as a cure for the headache. Coffee is supposed to act as a preventative of gravel and gout, and to its influence is ascribed the rarity of those diseases in France and Turkey. Both tea and coffee powerfully counteract the effects of opium and intoxicating liquors; though, when taken in excess, and without nourishing food, they themselves produce, temporarily at least, some of the more disagreeable consequences incident to the use of ardent spirits. In general, however, none but persons possessing great mobility of the nervous system, or enfeebled or effeminate constitutions, are injuriously affected by the moderate use of tea and coffee in connection with food.

Coffee.

One full coffeecupful of ground coffee, stirred with one egg and part of the shell, adding a half cupful of cold water. Put it into the coffee boiler, and pour on to it a quart of boiling water; as it rises and begins to boil, stir it down with a silver spoon or fork. Boil hard for ten or twelve minutes. Remove from the fire and pour out a cupful of coffee; then pour back into the coffeepot. Place it on the back of the stove or range where it will keep hot (and not boil); it will settle in about five minutes. Send to the table hot. Serve with good cream and lump sugar. Three-quarters of a pound of Java and a quarter of a pound of Mocha make the best mixture of coffee.

Buttermilk as a Drink.

Buttermilk, so generally regarded as a waste product, has latterly been coming somewhat into vogue, not only as a nutrient, but as a therapeutic agent, and in an editorial article the *Canada Lancet,* some time ago, highly extolled its virtues. Buttermilk may be roughly described as milk which has lost most of its fat and a small percentage of casein, and which has become sour by fermentation. Long experience has demonstrated it to be an agent of superior digestibility. It is, indeed, a true milk peptone—that is, milk already partly digested, the coagulation of the coagulable portion being loose and flaky, and not of that firm indigestible nature which is the result of the action of the gastric juice upon cow's sweet milk. It resembles koumiss in its nature, and, with the exception of that article, it is the most grateful, refreshing and digestible of the products of milk. It is a decided laxative to the bowels, a fact which must be borne in mind in the treatment of typhoid fever, and which may be turned to advantage in the treatment of habitual constipation. It is a diuretic, and may be prescribed with advantage in some kidney troubles. Owing to its acidity, combined with its laxative properties, it is believed to exercise a general impression on the liver. It is well adapted to many cases where it is customary to recommend lime water and milk. It is invaluable in the treatment of diabetes, either exclusively, or alternating with skimmed milk. In some cases of gastric ulcer and cancer of the stomach, it is the only food that can be retained.

$\bigstar$

$\mathcal{B}$REAKFAST

$\bigstar$

⊰ MEXICAN OMELET ⊱

*"As everybody knows, there is only one infallible recipe
for the perfect omelette: your own."—Elizabeth David*

2 cups liquid egg substitute

1 teaspoon salt, divided

1/4 teaspoon pepper, divided

1/4 cup skim milk

1 cup sliced fresh mushrooms

2 medium tomatoes, peeled and chopped

1 tablespoon liquid Butter Buds®

1/8 teaspoon garlic powder

1/4 avocado, peeled, seeded, and finely diced

Cooking spray

In a large bowl, whisk together egg substitute, 3/4 teaspoon salt, 1/8 teaspoon pepper, and milk. Set aside. In a small pan combine mushrooms, tomatoes, and Butter Buds. Sauté vegetables for 5 minutes over medium heat. Season with 1/4 teaspoon salt, 1/8 teaspoon pepper, and 1/8 teaspoon garlic powder. Remove from heat and toss in avocado.

To make omelet, coat large non-stick skillet with cooking spray. Heat pan. Pour in egg mixture. Quickly tilt pan, lifting edges of omelet to let egg liquid flow underneath. Return to stove and lower heat. When egg is firm, but moist on top, loosen edges. Sprinkle vegetables over half of omelet and fold other half over. May be served with salsa.

Preparation time: 25 minutes

NUTRIENT INFORMATION

Servings per recipe: 4 —Serving size: 1/4 omelet

*Protein 18 g, Carbohydrate 5 g, Fat 7 g, Saturated Fat 1 g,
Cholesterol 2 mg, Sodium 907 mg, Dietary Fiber 2 g*

*Calories 155
From protein: 46%; From carbohydrate: 13%; From fat: 41%*

Food Exchanges: 2 lean meat, 1 vegetable

VEGETABLE OMELET

from the White House Cookbook, 1894

Make a purée by mashing up ready-dressed vegetables, together with a little milk, cream or gravy and some seasoning. The most suitable vegetables are cucumbers, artichokes, onions, sorrel, green peas, tomatoes, lentils, mushrooms, asparagus tops, potatoes, truffles, or turnips. Prepare some eggs by beating them very light. Pour them into a nice hot frying pan, containing a spoonful of butter; spread the purée upon the upper side; and when perfectly hot, turn or fold the omelet together and serve. Or cold vegetables may be merely chopped small, then tossed in a little butter, and some beaten and seasoned eggs poured over.

QUICK ASPARAGUS QUICHE

Some may believe that "Real men don't eat quiche."—Bruce Feirstein
But this quiche will certainly tempt your taste buds!

Crust:

1 cup all-purpose flour

1/2 teaspoon salt

4 tablespoons reduced-fat stick margarine

3 tablespoons cold water

Cooking spray

Filling:

3/4 cup shredded fat-free cheddar cheese

3/4 cup shredded cheddar cheese

1 cup liquid egg substitute

1 cup evaporated skim milk

8 1/4-ounce can no-salt-added corn, drained

8 1/2-ounce can asparagus tips, rinsed and drained

1 cup chopped Canadian bacon

1 tablespoon instant chopped onion

1/2 teaspoon salt

Dash black pepper

First, prepare crust. Combine all crust ingredients in a bowl and stir with a fork until well mixed. Shape the dough into a ball and place between two sheets of wax paper that have been dusted with flour. Roll the dough into a circle large enough to fit a 9" pie pan. Coat pie pan with cooking spray and arrange crust in pan. Cut the edges to fit the pan. Cover the edge of the crust with foil so it does not burn during baking.

Next, prepare filling. In a small bowl combine cheeses. In a large bowl, beat egg substitute with evaporated milk. Stir in corn, asparagus, 1 cup of cheese, Canadian bacon, onion, and seasonings. Pour filling into pastry

crust. Sprinkle remaining 1/2 cup cheese on top. Bake at 375° for
45 minutes, or until knife inserted in center comes out clean. Remove
foil from crust the last 5 minutes of baking.

Preparation time: 35 minutes
Baking time: 45 minutes

N U T R I E N T   I N F O R M A T I O N

Servings per recipe: 8—Serving size: 1 slice (1/8 of quiche)

Protein 17 g, Carbohydrate 22 g, Fat 9 g, Saturated Fat 3 g,
Cholesterol 18 mg, Sodium 808 mg, Dietary Fiber 2 g

Calories 237
From protein: 29%; From carbohydrate: 37%; From fat: 34%

Food Exchanges: 1 starch, 1 high fat meat, 1 vegetable

A S P A R A G U S   O M E L E T

from the White House Cookbook, 1894

*B*oil, with a little salt, and until about half cooked,
eight or ten stalks of asparagus, and cut the eatable
part into rather small pieces; beat the egg and mix the asparagus
with them. Make the omelet. Omelet with parsley is made
by adding a little chopped parsley.

❉HARDY BRUNCH❉ BAKE

Who would ever dream of having stuffing for breakfast?
That is exactly what lends the flavor to this egg casserole! Try serving
our Fresh Fruit with Cheesecake Creme alongside it.

Cooking spray

2 cups herb-seasoned stuffing cubes

1/4 cup finely chopped onion

2 tablespoons liquid Butter Buds®

1/3 cup thinly sliced fresh mushrooms

5 ounces thinly sliced Canadian bacon, chopped

1 cup shredded, reduced-fat, sharp cheddar cheese

1 cup liquid egg substitute

2 cups skim milk

1/2 teaspoon dry mustard

1/2 teaspoon onion salt

Coat a 12" x 8" pan with cooking spray and cover bottom of pan with stuffing cubes. In a small sauce pan, sauté onion in Butter Buds. Sprinkle stuffing with onion, mushrooms, Canadian bacon, and cheese. In a separate bowl, whisk together egg substitute, milk, dry mustard, and onion salt; pour over stuffing mixture. Cover and refrigerate overnight, or at least 8 hours.

Remove from refrigerator and bake uncovered at 325° for one hour.
Let stand 10 minutes before serving.

Preparation time: 20 minutes
Chilling time: 8 hours
Baking time: 60 minutes
Standing time: 10 minutes

NUTRIENT INFORMATION

Servings per recipe: 8—Serving size: 1 slice (1/8 of casserole)

Protein 17 g, Carbohydrate 16 g, Fat 6 g, Saturated Fat 2 g, Cholesterol 22 mg,
Sodium 807 mg, Dietary Fiber <1 g

Calories 186
From protein: 37%; From carbohydrate: 34%; From fat: 29%

Food Exchanges: 1 starch, 2 lean meat

BAKED OMELET

from the White House Cookbook, 1894

*B*eat the whites and yolks of four or six eggs separately; add to the
yolks a small cup of milk, a tablespoonful of flour or cornstarch,
a teaspoonful of baking powder, one-half teaspoonful of salt, and
lastly, the stiff-beaten whites. Bake in a well-buttered pie-tin or plate
about half an hour in a steady oven. It should be served the moment
it is taken from the oven, as it is liable to fall. "

❧ Pull-Apart ❧ Caramel Nut Coffee Cake

A wonderful addition to your brunch buffet.
Each person can pull off their own piece.

Cooking spray

1/4 cup finely chopped walnuts

25-ounce package frozen roll dough

5 tablespoons light brown sugar

6 tablespoons reduced-fat stick margarine, melted

1 large box cook and serve butterscotch pudding mix

Coat bundt pan with cooking spray. Sprinkle bottom of pan with walnuts. Place dough balls evenly on top of walnuts. In a small bowl, mix brown sugar and melted margarine; pour over dough. Sprinkle pudding mix on top. Place wax paper over top of pan and set in cold oven to rise overnight. Bake at 350° for 30 minutes. Turn out of pan immediately.

Preparation time: 15 minutes
Standing time: 8 hours
Baking time: 30 minutes

Nutrient Information

Servings per recipe: 14—Serving size: 1 slice (1/14 of coffee cake)

Protein 5 g, Carbohydrate 43 g, Fat 7 g, Saturated Fat 1 g,
Cholesterol 3 mg, Sodium 500 mg, Dietary Fiber 1 g

Calories 255
From protein: 8%; From carbohydrate: 67%; From fat: 25%

Food Exchanges: 3 starch

Rusks (Unfermented)

from the White House Cookbook, 1894

Three cups of flour sifted, three teaspoonfuls of baking powder,
one teaspoonful of salt, three tablespoonfuls of sugar, two
tablespoonfuls of butter, three eggs, half a nutmeg grated and a
teaspoonful of ground cinnamon, two small cups of milk;
sift together salt, flour, sugar, and baking powder; rub in the butter
cold; add the milk, beaten eggs, and spices; mix into a soft dough,
break off pieces about as large as an egg, roll them under the hands
into round balls, rub the tops with sugar and water mixed, and
then sprinkle dry sugar over them. Bake immediately.

ᴥBLUEBERRYᴥ
TEACAKES

*Nice served with our Quick Asparagus Quiche or Hardy Brunch Bake.
Also great with a steamy cup of Kahlúa Cocoa or freshly brewed tea.*

Teacakes:

1/4 cup reduced-fat stick margarine

1 1/2 cups sugar

1/2 cup liquid egg substitute

1 teaspoon orange extract

1 1/2 teaspoons lemon extract

1 teaspoon vanilla extract

4 cups all-purpose flour

2 1/2 teaspoons baking powder

1/2 cup skim milk

3-ounce package dried blueberries

Cooking spray

Glaze:

2 cups sifted powdered sugar

2 tablespoons skim milk

2 teaspoons lemon juice concentrate

With an electric mixer cream margarine; gradually add sugar, beating well at medium speed. Add egg substitute 1/4 cup at a time, beating well after each addition. Add extracts and beat until well blended.

In a separate bowl, combine flour and baking powder; add to creamed mixture alternately with milk. Mix until just blended. Stir in blueberries until evenly dispersed throughout dough. Divide dough into four equal portions and wrap each in plastic wrap. Chill 2 hours.

Take one package of dough out of the refrigerator at a time to work with. On a well-floured surface, roll dough to 1/8 inch thickness. Cut dough with a 2-inch round cookie or biscuit cutter. Place teacakes on cookie sheet coated with cooking spray. Bake at 375° for 6-7 minutes, or until edges are golden. Place on cooling rack to cool.

While teacakes are baking, prepare the glaze. Sift the powdered sugar into a bowl; stir in milk and lemon juice until well blended. Drizzle over teacakes after they have cooled.

Preparation time: 30 minutes—Chilling time: 2 hours
Baking time: 6-7 minutes—Cooling time: 20 minutes

NUTRIENT INFORMATION

Servings per recipe: 42—Serving size: 1 teacake

Protein 2 g, Carbohydrate 23 g, Fat 1 g, Saturated Fat <1 g, Cholesterol <1 mg, Sodium 50 mg, Dietary Fiber 1 g

Calories 109
From protein: 7%; From carbohydrate: 84%; From fat: 8%

Food Exchanges: 1 starch, 1 fruit

BERRY TEACAKES
from the White House Cookbook, 1894

Nice little teacakes to be baked in muffin-rings are made of one cup of sugar, two eggs, one and a half cups of milk, one heaping tea-spoonful of baking powder, a piece of butter the size of an egg and flour sufficient to make a stiff batter. In this batter stir a pint bowl of fruit—any fresh are nice—or canned berries with the juice poured off. Serve while warm and they are a dainty addition to the tea-table. Eaten with butter.

❧ Branana Pancakes ❧ With Pineapple Sauce

The pineapple sauce is a nice alternative to maple syrup.
Leftover sauce can be served warm over frozen vanilla yogurt.

Pancakes:
7-ounce envelope bran muffin mix

1/4 cup liquid egg substitute

2/3 cup skim milk

1 tablespoon canola oil

1/2 banana, mashed

Pineapple Sauce:
20-ounce can crushed pineapple canned in juice, undrained

1/3 cup sugar

1 tablespoon instant tapioca

1 tablespoon honey

1/2 teaspoon lemon juice

1/4 teaspoon ground ginger

To prepare pancakes, place muffin mix in a bowl and make a well in the center. In a separate bowl, combine wet ingredients. Pour wet ingredients into muffin mix and stir until just moistened. Stir in banana.

To make each pancake, pour 1/4 cup batter on hot nonstick griddle sprayed generously with cooking spray. Turn pancakes when tops are bubbly and edges look cooked, after about 4 minutes.

To prepare sauce, combine all ingredients in a saucepan and let stand 5 minutes. Bring to boil over medium heat. Reduce heat and simmer uncovered for 2-3 minutes, or until thickened. Stir occasionally throughout cooking. Serve warm over the pancakes.

Preparation time: 20 minutes
Cooking time: 15 minutes

NUTRIENT INFORMATION

Servings per recipe: 6 pancakes, 8 pineapple sauce
Serving size: 1 pancake, 1/4 cup pineapple sauce

Protein 6 g, Carbohydrate 49 g, Fat 5 g, Saturated Fat <1 g,
Cholesterol 1 mg, Sodium 440 mg, Dietary Fiber 1 g

Calories 265
From protein: 9%; From carbohydrate: 74%; From fat: 17%

Food Exchanges: 2 starch, 1 fruit, 1 fat

WHEAT GRIDDLE CAKES
from the White House Cookbook, 1894

Three cups of flour, one teaspoonful of salt, three teaspoonfuls of baking powder sifted together; beat three eggs and add to three cupfuls of sweet milk, also a tablespoonful of melted butter; mix all into a smooth batter, as thick as will run in a stream from the lips of a pitcher. Bake on a well-greased, hot griddle, a nice light brown. Very good.

B READS

❧CHEESE CRINKLES❧

The fat in this old-time favorite makes it a special treat.
Our version is vastly reduced in fat from the original recipe.

7 tablespoons reduced-fat stick margarine, softened
4 ounces reduced-fat extra sharp cheddar cheese, shredded
1 cup crisp rice cereal
1 cup all-purpose flour
3 dashes cayenne pepper
Cooking spray

Mix the margarine and cheese together by hand in a large bowl. Add all of the other ingredients and mix together with a fork. Pinch off small pieces of dough and roll in 1/2 inch balls. Place on a baking sheet coated with cooking spray. Flatten each ball with a fork.

Bake at 375° for 17 minutes, or until golden.

Preparation time: 20 minutes—Baking time: 17 minutes

NUTRIENT INFORMATION:

Servings per recipe: 20—Serving size: 3

Protein 3 g, Carbohydrate 6 g, Fat 3 g, Saturated Fat 1 g,
Cholesterol 3 mg, Sodium 105 mg, Dietary Fiber <1 g

Calories 63
From protein: 19%; From carbohydrate: 38%; From fat: 43%

Food Exchanges: 1/2 starch

CAYENNE CHEESE STRAWS

from the White House Cookbook, 1894

A quarter of a pound of flour, two ounces butter, two ounces grated parmesan cheese, a pinch of salt and a few grains of cayenne pepper. Mix into a paste with the yolk of an egg. Roll out to the thickness of a silver quarter, about four or five inches long; cut into strips about a third of an inch wide, twist them as you would a paper spill and lay them on a baking-sheet slightly floured. Bake in a moderate oven until crisp, but they must not be the least brown. Serve cold, piled tastefully on a glass dish. You can make the straws of remnants of puff pastry, rolling in the grated cheese.

WHEAT BREAD

from the White House Cookbook, 1894

Sift the flour into a large bread-pan or bowl; make a hole in the middle of it, and pour in the yeast in the ratio of half a teacupful of yeast to two quarts of flour; stir the yeast lightly, then pour in your "wetting," either milk or water, as you choose,—which use warm in winter and cold in summer; if you use water as "wetting," dissolve in it a bit of butter of the size of an egg;—if you use milk, no butter is necessary; stir in the "wetting" very lightly, but do not mix all the flour in it; then cover the pan with a thick blanket or towel, and set it, in winter, in a warm place to rise. This is called "putting the bread in sponge." In summer the bread should not be wet over night. In the morning add a teaspoonful of salt and mix all the flour in the pan with the sponge, kneading it well; then let it stand two hours or more until it has risen quite light; then remove the dough to the molding-board and mold it for a long time, cutting it in pieces and molding them together again and again until the dough is elastic under the pressure of your hand, using as little flour as possible; then make it into loaves, and put the loaves into baking-tins. The loaves should come halfway up the pan, and they should be allowed to rise until the bulk is doubled. When the loaves are ready to put into the oven, the oven should be ready to receive them. It should be hot enough to brown a teaspoonful of flour in five minutes. The heat should be greater at the bottom than at the top of the oven, and the fire so arranged as to give sufficient strength of heat through the baking without being replenished.

Let them stand ten or fifteen minutes; prick them three or four times with a fork; bake in a quick oven from forty-five to sixty minutes.

If these directions are followed, you will obtain sweet, tender and wholesome bread. If by any mistake the dough becomes sour before you are ready to bake it, you can rectify it by adding a little dry super-carbonate of soda, molding the dough a long time to distribute the soda equally throughout the mass. All bread is better, if naturally sweet, without the soda; but sour bread you should never eat, if you desire good health.

Keep well covered in a tin box or large stone crock, which should be wiped out every day or two, and scalded and dried thoroughly in the sun once a week.

RUTH'S DILLY BREAD

"You can travel fifty thousand miles in America without once tasting a piece of good bread."—Henry Miller
This bread of ours is an exception. It can be made in the morning and ready for a luncheon by noon.

1 package active dry yeast

1/4 cup warm water

1 cup fat-free cottage cheese heated to lukewarm

2 tablespoons sugar

1 tablespoon reduced-fat stick margarine

1 tablespoon instant chopped onion

2 teaspoons dill seed

1 teaspoon salt

1/4 teaspoon baking soda

1 unbeaten egg

2 1/4 cups all-purpose flour

Cooking spray

1 tablespoon reduced-fat stick margarine, melted

1/8 teaspoon salt

Soften yeast in the warm water. In mixing bowl combine softened yeast with cottage cheese, sugar, margarine, onion, dill seed, salt, soda, and egg. Add flour gradually to form a stiff dough, beating well after each addition. (May add up to another 1/4 cup flour, if needed, to make dough stiff.) Cover, let rise in a warm place until the dough is light and doubled in size, about 50-60 minutes. Stir down, turn into a loaf pan well greased with cooking spray. Let rise in a warm place until light, about 30-40 minutes. Bake at 350° for 40-50 minutes. Cool 5 minutes; then turn out of pan. Brush with melted margarine and sprinkle with 1/8 teaspoon salt.

Preparation time: 20 minutes
Rising time: approximately 1 hour 30 minutes
Baking time: 40-50 minutes

NUTRIENT INFORMATION

Servings per recipe: 12—Serving size: 1 slice

Protein 6 g, Carbohydrate 21 g, Fat 2 g, Saturated Fat <1 g,
Cholesterol 20 mg, Sodium 305 mg, Dietary Fiber 1 g

Calories 126
From protein: 19%; From carbohydrate: 67%; From fat: 14%

Food Exchanges: 1 starch, 2 vegetable

"A morsel of genuine history is a thing so rare as to always be vaulable."
—*Thomas Jefferson, 1817*

SPIDER CORN-CAKE
from the White House Cookbook, 1894

Beat two eggs and one-fourth cup sugar together. Then add one cup sweet milk and one cup of sour milk in which you have dissolved one teaspoonful soda. Add a teaspoonful of salt. Then mix one and two-thirds cups of granulated corn meal and one-third cup flour with this. Put a spider or skillet on the range and when it is hot, melt in two tablespoonfuls of butter. Turn the spider so that the butter can run up on the sides of the pan. Pour in the corn-cake mixture and add one more cup of sweet milk, but do not stir afterwards. Put this in the oven and bake from twenty to thirty-five minutes. When done, there should be a streak of custard through it.

❧ CORNY CORNBREAD ❧

"Without bread all is misery"—William Cobbett
So whip up this quick and easy cornbread!

2 cups white cornmeal

3/4 cup all-purpose flour

3/4 teaspoon baking soda

2 1/2 teaspoons baking powder

1/8 teaspoon salt

2 tablespoons sugar

2 cups non-fat buttermilk

1/4 cup evaporated skim milk

3/4 cup liquid egg substitute

1/4 cup corn oil

8 3/4-ounce can no-salt-added corn, drained

1 tablespoon instant chopped onion

Cooking spray

*I*n a large mixing bowl, combine cornmeal, flour, baking soda, baking
powder, salt, and sugar. Make a hole in center of dry ingredients. In
a separate bowl, stir together milks, egg substitute, and oil; pour into hole
in dry ingredients. Mix just until moistened. Stir in corn and onion. Coat
an 8" x 8" pan with cooking spray; then pour in batter. Bake at 450° for
25 minutes or until golden brown. Serve warm.

Preparation time: 20 minutes—Baking time: 25 minutes

NUTRIENT INFORMATION

Servings per recipe: 9—Serving size: 1 square (1/9 of cornbread)

Protein 9 g, Carbohydrate 43 g, Fat 8 g, Saturated Fat 1 g,
Cholesterol 2 mg, Sodium 375 mg, Dietary Fiber 2 g

Calories 280
From protein: 13%; From carbohydrate: 61%; From fat: 26%

Food Exchanges: 3 starch, 1 fat

HINT OF HONEY BISCUITS

Enjoy the hint of sweetness honey adds to these biscuits.

3 tablespoons plus 1 teaspoon reduced-fat
stick margarine, cut into small pieces
2 cups self-rising flour
3/4 cup 1% buttermilk
3 tablespoons honey
Cooking spray

In a large mixing bowl, cut margarine into flour with
pastry blender until the mixture resembles coarse corn meal.
Add buttermilk and honey, then stir until dry ingredients are just moistened.
Turn dough onto a well-floured surface and knead 5 times.
Roll dough to 3/4 inch thickness and cut with a biscuit cutter.
Place on a baking sheet coated with cooking spray.
Bake at 450° for 10 minutes, or until golden.

Preparation time: 20 minutes—Baking time: 10 minutes

NUTRIENT INFORMATION

Servings per recipe: 12—Serving size: 1 biscuit

*Protein 3 g, Carbohydrate 20 g, Fat 2 g, Saturated Fat <1 g,
Cholesterol 1 mg, Sodium 317 mg, Dietary Fiber 3 g*

Calories 110
From protein: 11%; From carbohydrate: 73%; From fat: 16%

Food Exchanges: 1 starch, 1 vegetable

LIGHT BISCUIT N^{O.} 1

from the White House Cookbook, 1894

Take a piece of bread dough that will make about as many biscuits as you wish; lay it out rather flat in a bowl; break into it two eggs, half a cup of sugar, half a cup of butter; mix this thoroughly with enough flour to keep it from sticking to the hands and board. Knead it well for about fifteen or twenty minutes, make into small biscuits, place in a greased pan, and let them rise until about even with the top of the pan. Bake in a quick oven for about half an hour. These can be made in the form of rolls, which some prefer.

❧ORANGE MIST❧ MUFFINS

A sweet muffin that is so good some prefer to serve it as a light dessert. Try adding one teaspoon of grated orange rind to enhance the fresh orange flavor.

Muffins:

1 cup self-rising flour

1/4 cup brown sugar

1/4 cup liquid egg substitute

1/2 cup unsweetened orange juice

1/4 cup canola oil

1/2 teaspoon vanilla extract

Cooking spray

Topping:

1/4 cup sugar

1 1/2 tablespoons all-purpose flour

1/2 teaspoon ground cinnamon

1 1/2 tablespoons reduced-fat margarine

For muffins, combine flour and sugar in mixing bowl; make a well in the center. In a separate bowl, mix together egg substitute, orange juice, oil, and vanilla extract; pour into well in dry ingredients and stir just until moistened. Spoon into paper muffin cups coated with cooking spray. Fill muffin cups about two-thirds full. Bake at 400° for 8 minutes.

Meanwhile, prepare topping by mixing all four ingredients together with a pastry cutter, cutting the margarine into the other ingredients. Remove muffins from oven, sprinkle with topping and return to oven for 6 minutes more, or until edges of muffins are lightly browned.

Preparation time: 25 minutes—Baking time: 14 minutes

NUTRIENT INFORMATION

Servings per recipe: 12—Serving size: 1 muffin

Protein 2 g, Carbohydrate 18 g, Fat 6 g, Saturated Fat 1 g, Cholesterol <1 mg, Sodium 160 mg, Dietary Fiber 1 g

Calories 134
From protein: 6%; From carbohydrate: 54%; From fat: 40%

Food Exchanges: 1 starch, 1 fat

RAISED MUFFINS N^{O.} 2

from the White House Cookbook, 1894

Three pints of flour, three eggs, a piece of butter the size of an egg, two heaping teaspoonfuls of white sugar, one-half cake of compressed yeast and a quart of milk; warm the milk with the butter in it; cool a little, stir in the sugar and add a little salt; stir this gradually into the flour, then add the eggs well beaten; dissolve the yeast in half a cup of lukewarm water and add to the other ingredients; if the muffins are wanted for luncheon, mix them about eight o'clock in the morning; if for breakfast, set them at ten o'clock at night; when ready for baking, stir in half a teaspoonful of soda dissolved in a teaspoonful of hot water; butter the muffin-rings or gem-irons and bake in a quick oven.

SALADS AND SAUCES

HOLLANDAISE SAUCE

from the White House Cookbook, 1894

*H*alf a teacupful of butter, the juice of half a lemon, the yolks of two eggs, a speck of cayenne pepper, half a cupful of boiling water, half a teaspoonful of salt; beat the butter to a cream, add the yolks of eggs one by one; then the lemon juice, pepper and salt, beating all thoroughly; place the bowl in which is the mixture in a saucepan of boiling water; beat with an egg-beater until it begins to thicken which will be in about a minute; then add the boiling water, beating all the time; stir until it begins to thicken like soft custard; stir a few minutes after taking from the fire; be careful not to cook it too long. This is very nice with baked fish.

❈Homemade Dill❈ Hollandaise Sauce

"The green and gold of my delight—Asparagus with Hollandaise."
—Thomas Augustine Daly

2 tablespoons liquid Butter Buds®

1 tablespoon all-purpose flour

1 cup boiling water

1/2 cup liquid egg substitute, beaten

1/4 teaspoon salt

Juice of 1/2 small lemon

2 drops yellow food coloring (optional)

1/2 teaspoon dry dillweed

Dash cayenne pepper

Combine Butter Buds and flour in a sauce pan, mixing well. Add boiling water and cook over low heat, stirring constantly until thickened. In a small bowl, beat egg substitute, salt, and lemon juice together. Stir some of the hot mixture into the egg mixture and then slowly add the egg mixture to the hot mixture, stirring constantly. Cook, whisking constantly, until thickened. Whisk in food coloring, dillweed, and pepper. Best when served fresh from the stove! A nice addition to fish, chicken, broccoli, or asparagus.

Preparation time: 20 minutes

Nutrient Information

Servings per recipe: 6—Serving size: 1/4 cup

Protein 3 g, Carbohydrate 2 g, Fat 1 g, Saturated Fat <1 g,
Cholesterol <1 mg, Sodium 187 mg, Dietary Fiber <1 g

Calories 29
From protein: 41%; From carbohydrate: 28%; From fat: 31%

Food Exchanges: 1 very lean meat

⚜CRAN-ORANGE⚜ RELISH

Different and delicious! A nice complement to baked or smoked chicken, as well as to that Thanksgiving turkey.

2 medium oranges

24 ounces fresh cranberries

2 cups sugar

1/2 cup chopped walnuts

Quarter each unpeeled orange and remove seeds. Place 1/4 of cranberries and 1/4 of orange slices in food processor and process until evenly chopped. Empty food processor into a large bowl and repeat three more times until all of cranberries and orange slices are chopped. Stir in sugar and then walnuts. Refrigerate. Extras can be frozen for later use.

Preparation time: 20 minutes

NUTRIENT INFORMATION

Servings per recipe: 22—Serving size: 1/4 cup

Protein 1 g, Carbohydrate 24 g, Fat 2 g, Saturated Fat <1 g, Cholesterol 0, Sodium 9 mg, Dietary Fiber 1 g

Calories 118
From protein: 3%; From carbohydrate: 81%; From fat: 15%

Food Exchanges: 2 fruit

CRANBERRY SAUCE
from the White House Cookbook, 1894

One quart of cranberries, two cupfuls of sugar and a pint of water. Wash the cranberries, then put them on the fire with the water, but in a covered saucepan. Let them simmer until each cranberry bursts open; then remove the cover of the saucepan, add the sugar and let them all boil twenty minutes without the cover. The cranberries must never be stirred from the time they are placed on the fire. This is an unfailing recipe for a most delicious preparation of cranberries. Very fine with turkey and game.

❧ Q U E E N   O F   H E A R T S ❧
S A L A D

*Despite the fat in the dressing, this salad is still a family
favorite for birthday and other special occasion dinners.*

*"Let the salad-maker be a spendthrift for oil, a miser for vinegar,
a statesman for salt and a madman for mixing."*
—Spanish Proverb

Dressing:

1/4 cup canola oil

2/3 cup red wine vinegar

1 teaspoon dried Italian salad dressing mix

1 teaspoon seasoned salt

1 teaspoon chopped dried parsley

1 teaspoon dried whole oregano

1/4 teaspoon onion powder

1/8 teaspoon garlic powder

1 tablespoon grated Parmesan cheese

Salad:

4 cups torn green leaf lettuce

4 cups torn red leaf lettuce

6-ounce jar marinated artichoke hearts, drained and chopped

1/2 cup hearts of palm, drained and sliced

Combine dressing ingredients in a jar. Close jar and shake well. Chill overnight to allow flavors to blend. May double dressing recipe to keep extra on hand. Combine salad ingredients in a large bowl and toss with chilled dressing. Serve immediately.

Preparation time: 30 minutes—Chilling time for dressing: 8 hours

Nutrient Information

Servings per recipe: 8—Serving size: 1 1/2 cups

*Protein 2 g, Carbohydrate 4 g, Fat 8 g, Saturated Fat 1 g,
Cholesterol 1 mg, Sodium 317 mg, Dietary Fiber 2 g*

Calories 96
From protein: 8%; From carbohydrate: 17%; From fat: 75%

Food Exchanges: 1 vegetable, 2 fat

MIXED SUMMER SALAD

from the White House Cookbook, 1894

Three heads of lettuce, two teaspoonfuls of green mustard leaves, a handful of water cresses, five tender radishes, one cucumber, three hard-boiled eggs, two teaspoonfuls of white sugar, one teaspoonful of salt, one teaspoonful of pepper, one teaspoonful of made mustard, one teacupful of vinegar, half a teacupful of oil.

Mix all well together, and serve with a lump of ice in the middle.

CHICKEN SALAD
from the White House Cookbook, 1894

*B*oil the fowls tender and remove all the fat, gristle and skin; mince the meat in small pieces, but do not hash it. To one chicken put twice and a half its weight in celery, cut in pieces of about one-quarter of an inch; mix thoroughly and set it in a cool place—the ice chest.

In the meantime prepare a "Mayonnaise dressing," and when ready for the table pour this dressing over the chicken and celery, tossing and mixing it thoroughly. Set it in a cool place until ready to serve. Garnish with celery tips, or cold hard-boiled eggs, lettuce leaves, from the heart, cold boiled beets or capers, olives.

Crisp cabbage is a good substitute for celery; when celery is not to be had, use celery vinegar in the dressing. Turkey makes a fine salad.

CURRY CHICKEN SALAD

"Chicken salad has a certain glamour about it. Like the little black dress, it is chic and adaptable anywhere."—Laurie Colwin

6.9-ounce package chicken-flavored rice and vermicelli mix, prepared as directed on package except for decreasing margarine to 1 tablespoon reduced-fat margarine

2/3 cup fat-free Italian dressing

12-ounce jar marinated artichoke hearts, drained and chopped

2 cups cooked chicken breast, chopped

6-ounce can water chestnuts, drained and chopped

1/2 cup chopped green onions

3/4 cup reduced-fat mayonnaise

1 tablespoon curry powder

1 teaspoon black pepper

Place freshly cooked rice and vermicelli mix in a large bowl. Stir in fat-free Italian dressing. Cool. To rice mixture, add artichoke hearts, chicken, water chestnuts, and onions. In a separate bowl, combine mayonnaise, curry powder, and pepper. Stir into chicken and rice mixture. Cover and chill 1 1/2 hours.

Preparation time: 40 minutes (including cooking time for rice and chicken)
Chilling time: 1 hour 30 minutes

NUTRIENT INFORMATION

Servings per recipe: 7—Serving size: 3/4 cup

Protein 12 g, Carbohydrate 23 g, Fat 9 g, Saturated Fat 1 g, Cholesterol 30 mg, Sodium 765 mg, Dietary Fiber 2 g

Calories 221
From protein: 22%; From carbohydrate: 42%; From fat: 37%

Food Exchanges: 1 starch, 1 vegetable, 1 lean meat, 1 fat

❧FAY'S FREEZER❧ COLE SLAW

Try this colorful, crunchy cole slaw at your next picnic!

1 medium cabbage, chopped (about 8 cups)

1 teaspoon salt

1 carrot, peeled and grated

1/2 green pepper, chopped

1/2 red pepper, chopped

1/4 cup warm water

1 3/4 cups sugar

1 cup vinegar

1 teaspoon celery seed

4 teaspoons whole mustard seed

*M*ix cabbage and salt and let stand for 1 hour; then add carrot and peppers to the cabbage. Combine water, sugar, vinegar, and celery seed in saucepan and boil one minute. Cool and pour over cabbage mixture. Stir to coat. Spoon into 1-pint containers and add 1 teaspoon whole mustard seed to each container. Freeze. Thaw and serve, as needed.

Preparation time: 20 minutes—Standing time: 60 minutes

NUTRIENT INFORMATION

Servings per recipe: 16—Serving size: 1/2 cup

Protein 1 g, Carbohydrate 27 g, Fat <1 g, Saturated Fat <1 g, Cholesterol 0, Sodium 154 mg, Dietary Fiber 2 g

Calories 117
From protein: 3%; From carbohydrate: 92%; From fat: 4%

Food Exchanges: 1 starch, 1 vegetable

COLD SLAW

from the White House Cookbook, 1894

Select the finest head of bleached cabbage—that is to say, one of the finest and most compact of the more delicate varieties; cut up enough into shreds to fill a large vegetable dish or salad bowl—that to be regulated by the size of the cabbage and the quantity required; shave very fine and after that chop up, the more thoroughly the better. Put this into a dish in which it is to be served, after seasoning it well with salt and pepper. Turn over it a dressing made as for cold slaw; mix it well and garnish with slices of hard-boiled eggs.

POTATO SALAD, COLD

from the White House Cookbook, 1894

Chop cold boiled potatoes fine, with enough raw onions
to season nicely; make a dressing as for lettuce salad, and
pour over it.

❧ HORSERADISH ☙ POTATO SALAD

The horseradish provides a delicious twist to a traditional recipe.

1/2 cup fat-free mayonnaise

1/2 cup plain nonfat yogurt

2 teaspoons prepared mustard

2 teaspoons prepared horseradish

1 tablespoon chopped chives

1/4 teaspoon salt

1/8 teaspoon black pepper

2 cups potatoes, peeled, cooked, and cubed

1/4 cup diced celery

1/2 medium cucumber, peeled and diced

1 boiled egg, diced

1 boiled egg white, diced

*I*n a large bowl combine mayonnaise, yogurt, mustard, horseradish, and spices. Add remaining ingredients and toss well. Refrigerate until chilled, at least one hour.

Preparation time: 30 minutes—Chilling time: 60 minutes

NUTRIENT INFORMATION

Servings per recipe: 6—Serving size: 1/2 cup

Protein 5 g, Carbohydrate 22 g, Fat 1 g, Saturated Fat <1 g, Cholesterol 36 mg, Sodium 440 mg, Dietary Fiber 1 g

Calories 117
From protein: 17%; From carbohydrate: 75%; From fat: 8%

Food Exchanges: 1 starch, 1 vegetable

☀BOUNTIFUL☀
BEAN SALAD

A quick and fiber-rich dish for potlucks!

16-ounce can garbanzo beans, drained and rinsed

14-1/2 ounce can no-salt-added French-style green beans, drained

12-ounce jar marinated artichoke hearts, drained and quartered

3/4 cup fat-free Italian dressing

Combine first three ingredients in a large bowl. Pour dressing over vegetables and toss gently. Cover and chill 2 hours.

Preparation time: 10 minutes—Chilling time: 2 hours

NUTRIENT INFORMATION

Servings per recipe: 12—Serving size: 1/2 cup

Protein 2 g, Carbohydrate 10 g, Fat 2 g, Saturated Fat <1 g, Cholesterol 0, Sodium 368 mg, Dietary Fiber 3 g

Calories 66
From protein: 12%; From carbohydrate: 61%; From fat: 27%

Food Exchanges: 2 vegetable

BEAN SALAD

from the White House Cookbook, 1894

String young beans; break into half-inch pieces or leave whole; wash and cook soft in salt water; drain well; add finely chopped onions, pepper, salt and vinegar; when cool, add olive oil or melted butter.

PICKLED MUSHROOMS
from the White House Cookbook, 1894

Sufficient vinegar to cover the mushrooms; to each quart of mush-rooms two blades pounded mace, one ounce ground pepper, salt to taste. Choose some nice young button mushrooms for pickling and rub off the skin with a piece of flannel and salt, and cut off the stalks; if very large, take out the red inside, and reject the black ones, as they are too old. Put them in a stewpan, sprinkle salt over them, with pounded mace and pepper in the above proportion; shake them well over a clear fire until the liquor flows and keep them there until it is all dried up again; then add as much vinegar as will cover them; just let it simmer for one minute and store it away in stone jars for use. When cold, tie down with bladder and keep in a dry place; they will remain good for a length of time, and are generally considered excellent for flavoring stews and other dishes.

⁂Overnight⁂ Marinated Mushrooms

"Life is too short to stuff a mushroom."—Shirley Connan
So marinate one with our recipe!

3/4 cup red wine vinegar

1/4 cup canola oil

2 tablespoons lemon juice

1 teaspoon tarragon

3 teaspoons chopped chives

1 teaspoon minced garlic

1 teaspoon salt

1/8 teaspoon black pepper

1/2 teaspoon sugar

5 cups small mushrooms

Combine all ingredients except mushrooms, stirring well. Place mushrooms in container with lid. Pour marinade over mushrooms, coating well. Marinate in the refrigerator overnight, or at least 8 hours. Stir two or three times while marinating. Drain and serve.

Preparation time: 15 minutes—Chilling time: 8 hours

Nutrient Information

Servings per recipe: 20—Serving size: 1/4 cup

Protein 1 g, Carbohydrate 1 g, Fat 1 g, Saturated Fat <1 g,
Cholesterol 0, Sodium 28 mg, Dietary Fiber <1 g

Calories 17
From protein: 24%; From carbohydrate: 24%; From fat: 53%*

Food Exchanges: free

* Note: Although these mushrooms contain only 1 gram of fat per serving, the percent of calories from fat is high because oil is the only significant calorie source.

✦ GRAN'S PICKLED ✦ EGGS

Finally something to do with those leftover Easter eggs! Yummy by themselves or with a sandwich. The yolk contributes the fat and cholesterol to this delicacy.

1 cup cider vinegar

1/2 cup sugar

1/2 cup water

1 teaspoon pickling spice

1 cup juice from pickled beets

2-3 drops red food coloring

6 boiled eggs, shell removed

In a container with a lid, mix together all ingredients except eggs. The container needs to be deep enough so that the eggs will be completely immersed in the liquid. Add eggs and cover tightly. Refrigerate. Eggs will be pickled and ready to eat in 10 days. This recipe can be easily doubled or tripled for more eggs.

Preparation time: 25 minutes (including cooking time for eggs)
Standing time: 10 days

NUTRIENT INFORMATION

Servings per recipe: 6—Serving size: 1 egg

Protein 6 g, Carbohydrate 10 g, Fat 5 g, Saturated Fat 2 g,
Cholesterol 213 mg, Sodium 62 mg, Dietary Fiber 0

Calories 109
From protein: 22%; From carbohydrate: 37%; From fat: 41%

Food Exchanges: 2 vegetable, 1 medium fat meat

PICKLED EGGS

from the White House Cookbook, 1894

*P*ickled eggs are very easily prepared and most excellent as an accompaniment for cold meats. Boil quite hard three dozen eggs, drop in cold water and remove the shells, and pack them when entirely cold in a wide-mouthed jar, large enough to let them in or out without breaking. Take as much vinegar as you think will cover them entirely, and boil it in white pepper, allspice, a little root ginger; pack them in stone or wide-mouthed glass jars, occasionally putting in a tablespoonful of white and black mustard seed mixed, a small piece of race ginger, garlic, if liked, horse-radish ungrated, whole cloves, and a very little allspice. Slice two or three green peppers, and add in very small quantities. They will be fit for use in eight or ten days.

SALAD OF MIXED FRUITS

from the White House Cookbook, 1894

Put in the centre of a dish a pineapple properly pared, cored and sliced, yet retaining as near as practicable its original shape. Peel, quarter, and remove the seeds from four sweet oranges; arrange them in a border around the pineapple. Select four fine bananas, and peel and cut into slices lengthwise; arrange these zigzag-fence fashion around the border of the dish. In the V-shaped spaces around the dish, put tiny mounds of grapes of mixed colors. When complete, the dish should look very appetizing. To half a pint of clear sugar syrup add half an ounce of good brandy; pour over the fruit and serve.

⁂FRESH FRUIT WITH⁂ CHEESECAKE CREME

A colorful start or finish to a special meal.

Fruit:

2 cups halved seedless purple grapes

2 cups watermelon cubes

2 cups quartered strawberries

2 cups mandarin orange slices, drained

2 kiwi, peeled and sliced

1 banana, sliced

Cheesecake Creme:

4 ounces fat-free cream cheese

3 1/2 ounces marshmallow cream

1 1/2 teaspoons grated orange rind

Dash ginger

Combine all fruit, except banana, in a large bowl and toss gently. Cover and chill one hour, if desired. Right before serving add banana and toss. While fruit is chilling, make cheesecake creme. Combine cream cheese and marshmallow cream in a mixing bowl. With an electric mixer, beat until fluffy. Add orange rind and ginger; whip until well mixed. May chill, if desired, to allow flavors to blend. To serve, spoon fruit into small bowl and top with 2 tablespoons cheesecake creme.

Preparation time: 30 minutes—Chilling Time: 60 minutes

NUTRIENT INFORMATION

Servings per recipe: 11—Serving size: 1 cup fruit, 2 tablespoons cheesecake creme

*Protein 3 g, Carbohydrate 25 g, Fat 1 g, Saturated Fat <1 g,
Cholesterol 0, Sodium 69 mg, Dietary Fiber 2 g*

*Calories 121
From protein: 10%; From carbohydrate: 83%; From fat: 7%*

Food Exchanges: 2 fruit

Excerpted from the original
WHITE HOUSE COOKBOOK
1894

Catsups and Vinegars.

Tomato Catsup. No. 1.

Put into two quarts of tomato pulp (or two cans of canned tomatoes), one onion, cut fine, two tablespoonfuls of salt, and three tablespoonfuls of brown sugar. Boil until quite thick; then take from the fire and strain it through a sieve, working it until it is all through but the seeds. Put it back on the stove, and add two tablespoonfuls of mustard, one of allspice, one of black pepper, and one of cinnamon, one teaspoonful of ground cloves, half a teaspoonful of cayenne pepper, one grated nutmeg, one pint of good vinegar; boil it until it will just run from the mouth of a bottle. It should be watched, stirred often, that it does not burn. If sealed tight while hot, in large-mouthed bottles, it will keep good for years.

Tomato Catsup. No. 2.

Cook one gallon of choice ripe tomatoes; strain them, and cook again until they become quite thick. About fifteen minutes before taking up, put into them a small level teaspoonful of cayenne pepper, one tablespoonful of mustard seed, half a tablespoonful of whole cloves, one tablespoonful of whole allspice, all tied in a thin muslin bag. At the same time, add one heaping table-spoonful of sugar, and one teacupful of best vinegar, and salt to suit the taste. Seal up air-tight, either in bottles or jugs. This is a valuable Southern recipe.

Green Tomato Catsup.

One peck of green tomatoes and two large onions sliced. Place them in layers, sprinkling salt between; let them stand twenty-four hours and then drain them. Add a quarter of a pound of mustard seed, one ounce allspice, one ounce cloves, one ounce ground mustard, one ounce ground ginger, two tablespoonfuls black pepper, two teaspoonfuls celery seed, a quarter of a pound of brown sugar. Put all in preserving-pan, cover with vinegar, and boil two hours; then strain through a sieve and bottle for use.

Walnut Catsup.

One hundred walnuts, six ounces of shallots, one head of garlic, half a pound of salt, two quarts of vinegar, two ounces of anchovies, two ounces of pepper, a quarter of an ounce of mace, half an ounce of cloves; beat in a large mortar, a hundred green walnuts until they are thoroughly broken; then put them into a jar with six ounces of shallots cut into pieces, a head of garlic, two quarts of vinegar and the half pound of salt; let them stand for a fort-night, stirring them twice a day. Strain off the liquor, put into a stewpan with the anchovies, whole pepper, half an ounce of cloves and a quarter of an ounce of mace; boil it half an hour, skimming it well. Strain it off, and, when cold, pour it clear from any sediment into small bottles, cork it down closely and store it in a dry place. The sediment can be used for flavoring sauces.

Oyster Catsup.

One pint of oyster meats, one teacupful of sherry, a tablespoonful of salt, a teaspoonful of cayenne pepper, the same of powdered mace, a gill of cider vinegar.

Procure the oysters very fresh and open sufficient to fill a pint measure; save the liquor and scald the oysters in it with the sherry; strain the oysters and chop them fine with the salt, cayenne, and mace until reduced to a pulp; then add it to the liquor in which they were scalded; boil it again five minutes and skim well; rub the whole through a sieve, and when cold, bottle and cork closely. The corks should be sealed.

Mushroom Catsup.

Use the larger kind known as umbrellas or "flaps." They must be very fresh and not gathered in very wet weather, or the catsup will be less apt to keep. Wash and cut them in two to four pieces, and place them in a wide, flat jar or crock in layers, sprinkling each layer with salt, and let them stand for twenty-four hours; take them out and press out the juice; then bottle and cork; put the mushrooms back again, and in another twenty-four hours press them again; bottle and cork; repeat this for the third time, and then mix together all the juice extracted; add to it pepper, allspice, one or more cloves according to quantity, pounded together; boil the whole, and skim as long as any scum rises; bottle when cool; put in a dry place, and it will keep for years.

Gooseberry Catsup.

Ten pounds of fruit gathered just before ripening, five pounds of sugar, one quart of vinegar, two tablespoonfuls each of ground black pepper, all-spice, and cinnamon. Boil the fruit in vinegar until reduced to a pulp, and then add sugar and the other seasoning. Seal it hot.

Grape catsup is made in the same manner.

Cucumber Catsup.

Take cucumbers suitable for the table; peel and grate them, salt a little, and put in a bag to drain over night; in the morning, season to taste with salt, pepper and vinegar; put in small jars and seal tight for fall or winter use.

Currant Catsup.

Four pounds of currants, two pounds of sugar, one pint of vinegar, one teaspoonful of cloves, a tablespoonful of cinnamon, pepper, and allspice. Boil in a porcelain saucepan until thoroughly cooked. Strain through a sieve all but the skins; boil down until just thick enough to run freely from the mouth of a bottle when cold. Cork and set aside.

Apple Catsup.

Peel and quarter a dozen sound, tart apples; stew them until soft in as little water as possible, then pass them through a sieve. To a quart of the sift-ed apple, add a teacupful of sugar, one teaspoonful of pepper, one of cloves, one of mustard, two of cinnamon, and two medium-sized onions, chopped very fine. Stir all together, adding a tablespoonful of salt and a pint of vinegar. Place over the fire and boil one hour, and bottle while hot; seal very tight. It should be about as thick as tomato catsup, so that it will just run from the bottle.

Celery Vinegar.

A quart of fresh celery, chopped fine, or a quarter of a pound of celery seed; one quart of best vinegar; one tablespoonful of salt, and one of white sugar. Put the celery or seed into a jar; heat the vinegar, sugar and salt; pour it boiling hot over the celery, let it cool, cover it tightly, and set away. In two weeks strain and bottle.

Spiced Vinegar.

Take one quart of cider vinegar, put into it half an ounce of celery seed, one-third of an ounce of dried mint, one-third of an ounce of dried parsley, one garlic, three small onions, three whole cloves, a teaspoonful of whole pepper-corns, a teaspoonful of grated nutmeg, salt to taste, and a table-spoonful of sugar; add a tablespoonful of good brandy. Put all into a jar, and cover it well; let it stand for three weeks, then strain and bottle it well. Useful for flavoring salad and other dishes.

SOUPS

CHICKEN CREAM SOUP

from the White House Cookbook, 1894

*A*n old chicken for soup is much the best. Cut it up into quarters, put it into a soup kettle with half a pound of corned ham and an onion; add four quarts of cold water. Bring slowly to a gentle boil, and keep this up until the liquid has diminished one-third, and the meat drops from the bones; then add half a cup of rice. Season with salt, pepper, and a bunch of chopped parsley.

Cook slowly until the rice is tender; then the meat should be taken out. Now stir in two cups of rich milk thickened with a little flour. The chicken could be fried in a spoonful of butter and a gravy made, reserving some of the white part of the meat, chopping it and adding it to the soup.

❧ CLASSIC CREAMY ❧ CHICKEN SOUP

"Of soup and love, the first is best."—Spanish Proverb

3 cups low-sodium chicken bouillon

2 cups shredded, cooked chicken breast

1 tablespoon instant chopped onion

3 tablespoons liquid Butter Buds®

1/3 cup all-purpose flour

1/4 teaspoon salt

1/8 teaspoon black pepper

1/2 cup evaporated skim milk

1/2 cup cooked rice

6 tablespoons seasoned stuffing mix

6 tablespoons chopped parsley

Place bouillon, chicken, and onion in a 2-quart pan. Bring to a boil. Meanwhile, place Butter Buds in a 2-cup glass measure. Add flour, salt, and pepper; mix well with wire whisk. Add 1 cup of the hot broth to flour mixture, blending well with wire whisk to remove lumps. Return flour mixture to broth. Over medium heat, stir with whisk until thickened. Stir in evaporated skim milk and rice; then heat 5 minutes. Spoon into bowls and top each serving with one tablespoon seasoned stuffing mix and chopped parsley.

Preparation time: 40 minutes (including cooking time for rice and chicken)

NUTRIENT INFORMATION

Servings per recipe: 6—Serving size: 1 cup

Protein 16 g, Carbohydrate 14 g, Fat 3 g, Saturated Fat 1 g, Cholesterol 33 mg, Sodium 278 mg, Dietary Fiber <1 g

Calories 150
From protein: 44%; From carbohydrate: 38%; From fat: 18%

Food Exchanges: 1 starch, 2 very lean meat

☙ TAMI'S WHITE ❧ BEAN SOUP

A family favorite on frosty winter nights.
Serve with a tossed salad and whole wheat rolls.

2 (15-ounce) cans navy beans, drained and rinsed

2 (14 1/2-ounce) cans low-sodium chicken broth

1 cup water

1 1/4 cups chopped onion

1 clove garlic, minced

2 cups shredded, cooked chicken breast

1 teaspoon ground cumin

3/4 teaspoon whole oregano

1/2 teaspoon cayenne pepper

4-ounce can chopped green chilies

1/2 cup plus 2 tablespoons shredded, reduced-fat Monterey Jack cheese

Combine beans, broth, water, onion, and garlic in large pan. Add chicken, spices, and chilies. Cover and cook over medium heat 30 minutes. If thicker soup is desired, remove lid from pan and cook longer. Spoon into bowls and top each with 1 tablespoon cheese. Delicious leftover!

Preparation time: 60 minutes (including cooking time for chicken)

NUTRIENT INFORMATION

Servings per recipe: 10—Serving size: 1 cup

Protein 17 g, Carbohydrate 20 g, Fat 3 g, Saturated Fat 1 g,
Cholesterol 24 mg, Sodium 353 mg, Dietary Fiber 1 g

Calories 175
From protein: 39%; From carbohydrate: 46%; From fat: 15%

Food Exchanges: 1 starch, 1 vegetable, 1 lean meat

DRIED BEAN SOUP
from the White House Cookbook, 1894

Put two quarts of dried white beans to soak the night before you make the soup, which should be put on as early in the day as possible. Take two pounds of the lean of fresh beef—the coarse pieces will do. Cut them up and put them into your soup-pot with the bones belonging to them (which should be broken in pieces), and a pound of lean bacon, cut very small. If you have the remains of a piece of beef that has been roasted the day before, and so much under-done that the juices remain in it, you may put it into the pot and its bones along with it. Season the meat with pepper only, and pour on it six quarts of water. As soon as it boils, take off the scum, and put in the beans (having first drained them) and a head of celery cut small, or a tablespoonful of pounded celery seed. Boil it slowly till the meat is done to shreds, and the beans all dissolved. Then strain it through a colander into the tureen, and put into it small squares of toasted bread with the crust cut off.

MULLAGATAWNY SOUP
(AS MADE IN INDIA)

from the White House Cookbook, 1894

Cut four onions, one carrot, two turnips, and one head of celery into three quarts of liquor, in which one or two fowls have been boiled; keep it over a brisk fire till it boils, and then place it on a corner of the fire, and let it simmer twenty minutes; add one table-spoonful of currie powder, and one tablespoonful of flour; mix the whole well together, and let it boil three minutes; pass it through a colander; serve with pieces of roast chicken in it; add boiled rice in a separate dish. It must be of good yellow color, and not too thick. If you find it too thick, add a little boiling water and a teaspoonful of sugar. Half veal and half chicken answers as well.

A dish of rice, to be served separately with this soup, must be thus prepared: put three pints of water in a saucepan and one tablespoon-ful of salt; let this boil. Wash well, in three waters, half a pound of rice; strain it, and put it into the boiling water in saucepan. After it has come to the boil—which it will do in about two minutes—let it boil twenty minutes; strain it through a colander, and pour over it two quarts of cold water. This will separate the grains of rice. Put it back in the saucepan, and place it near the fire until hot enough to send to the table. This is also the proper way to boil rice for curries. If these directions are strictly carried out every grain of the rice will separate, and be thoroughly cooked.

☙My Mullagatawny☙

Not hard to make, but takes time and is well worth it!

Cooking spray

1 teaspoon olive oil

1 1/2 cups chopped onion

2 cloves garlic, minced

1 tablespoon curry powder

5 (14 1/2-ounce) cans low-sodium chicken broth

4 cups water

1 1/3 cups dried lentils, washed

1 stalk celery, finely diced

1 carrot, peeled and finely diced

1/4 teaspoon salt

1/4 cup lime juice

2 cups shredded, cooked chicken breast

3 1/2 cups cooked rice

2 tablespoons plus 1 teaspoon fat-free sour cream

Coat a large pan with cooking spray; add oil and place over medium heat until oil is hot. Add onion, garlic, and curry powder; sauté 1 minute. Add broth, water, lentils, celery, carrot, and salt; bring to a boil. Reduce heat and simmer covered for 2 hours, stirring occasionally. Stir in lime juice. With a potato masher, mash lentils until soup is desired thickness. Stir in cooked chicken and simmer 15 minutes. Place 1/2 cup rice in each soup bowl and ladle 1 cup mullagatawny over rice. Top with 1 teaspoon fat-free sour cream.

Preparation time: 2 hours 30 minutes (including cooking time for chicken and rice)

Nutrient Information

Servings per recipe: 7—Serving size: 1 cup mullagatawny, 1/2 cup rice

Protein 21 g, Carbohydrate 43 g, Fat 5 g, Saturated Fat 2 g,
Cholesterol 28 mg, Sodium 182 mg, Dietary Fiber 2 g

Calories 301
From protein: 28%; From carbohydrate: 57%; From fat: 15%

Food Exchanges: 2 starch, 2 lean meat, 2 vegetable

☆SPICY SEAFOOD☆ GUMBO

If you've never had seafood gumbo, you're in for a real treat!

Spice Mix:

1 teaspoon cayenne pepper

1 1/2 teaspoons paprika

1 teaspoon chopped dried parsley

1/2 teaspoon thyme

1/4 teaspoon ground oregano

1 teaspoon salt

1 teaspoon black pepper

Gumbo:

3/4 cup low-sodium chicken bouillon

2 cups finely chopped celery

2 cups chopped onions

3 tablespoons gumbo filé powder

1 teaspoon minced garlic

15-ounce can tomato sauce

4 cups bottled clam juice

1 cup no-salt-added chicken bouillon

2 cups frozen chopped okra, thawed

2 cups packed, canned chunk crab meat, drained

2 (6 1/2-ounce) cans minced clams, drained

8 ounce frozen precooked baby shrimp, thawed

2 1/4 cups cooked white rice

In a small bowl, combine spice mix ingredients and set aside. In a stock pot, combine 3/4 cup chicken bouillon, celery, and onions. Sauté over medium heat for 10 minutes. Stir in gumbo filé powder, garlic, and spice mix. Turn heat to high and cook for 5 minutes, stirring constantly to prevent sticking as ingredients become very thick. Add clam

G U M B O
O R O K R A S O U P

from the White House Cookbook, 1894

---

*F*ry out the fat of a slice of bacon or fat ham, drain it off,
and in it fry the slices of a large onion brown; scald, peel
and cut up two quarts fresh tomatoes when in season (use canned
tomatoes otherwise), and cut thin one quart okra; put them,
together with a little chopped parsley, in a stew-kettle with about
three quarts of hot broth of any kind; cook slowly for three hours,
season with salt and pepper. Serve hot.

In chicken broth the same quantity of okra pods, used for
thickening instead of tomatoes, forms a chicken gumbo soup.

---

juice, remaining 1 cup bouillon, and okra; bring to a boil. Reduce heat
and simmer 40 minutes, stirring occasionally. Add crab, clams, and
shrimp, cover pot, and turn off heat. Let pot sit covered for 8-10 minutes,
or until seafood is just warmed. Serve at once. Spoon 1/4 cup rice into
each bowl and top with 1 cup gumbo.

Note:
Cooked seafood may also be used in place of canned or frozen seafood.

Preparation time: 1 hour 25 minutes

NUTRIENT INFORMATION

Servings per recipe: 9—Serving size: 1/4 cup rice, 1 cup gumbo

*Protein 19 g, Carbohydrate 22 g, Fat 2 g, Saturated Fat 1 g,
Cholesterol 101 mg, Sodium 914 mg, Dietary Fiber 2 g*

Calories 182
From protein: 42%; From carbohydrate: 48%; From fat: 10%

Food Exchanges: 1 starch, 1 vegetable, 2 very lean meat

SPRING VEGETABLE SOUP

from the White House Cookbook, 1894

*H*alf pint green peas, two shredded lettuces, one onion, a small bunch of parsley, two ounces butter, the yolks of three eggs, one pint of water, one and a half quarts of soup stock. Put in a stew-pan the lettuce, onion, parsley, and butter, with one pint of water, and let them simmer till tender. Season with salt and pepper. When done, strain off the vegetables, and put two-thirds of the liquor with the stock. Beat up the yolks of the eggs with the other third, toss it over the fire, and at the moment of serving add this with the vegetables to the strained-off soup.

☆More for Less☆ Vegetable Soup

Enjoy more taste for less fat with this colorful soup.

14 1/4-ounce can no-salt-added French-style green beans, drained

8 1/4-ounce can no-salt-added peas, drained

8 3/4-ounce can no-salt-added corn, drained

14 1/2-ounce can diced tomatoes

1 small onion, chopped

3 carrots, peeled and diced

2 stalks celery, diced

1/4 teaspoon black pepper

8 cups low-sodium chicken bouillon

8-ounce bag chopped cabbage

2 cups shredded, cooked chicken breast (optional)

1 cup cooked brown rice

1 tablespoon chopped dried parsley

Combine first seven vegetables, pepper, and bouillon in large stock pot; bring slowly to a boil. Reduce heat and simmer uncovered one hour, or until vegetables are tender. Add cabbage, chicken, rice, and parsley; simmer 20 minutes.

Preparation time: 1 hour 35 minutes (including cooking time for chicken and rice)

Nutrient Information
(including chicken)

Servings per recipe: 12—Serving size: 1 cup

*Protein 10 g, Carbohydrate 14 g, Fat 3 g, Saturated Fat 1 g,
Cholesterol 16 mg, Sodium 136 mg, Dietary Fiber 2 g*

*Calories 123
From protein: 33%; From carbohydrate: 46%; From fat: 22%*

Food Exchanges: 3 vegetable, 1 very lean meat

☙RICH POTATO❧ BROCCOLI SOUP

The two vegetables in this soup pack a vitamin C-rich punch!

4 1/2 cups peeled and cubed potatoes

5 cups water

3 packets low-sodium chicken bouillon granules

1 cup chopped onion

1 tablespoon liquid Butter Buds®

10 ounces frozen chopped broccoli, thawed and drained

1/2 teaspoon salt

1/2 teaspoon black pepper

6 ounces reduced-fat shredded cheddar cheese

In a large pot, place potatoes, water, and bouillon. Cook potatoes until tender. While potatoes are cooking, sauté onion in Butter Buds in a separate pan. When potatoes are tender, mash one-third with a potato masher. Add sautéed onion and broccoli to potatoes. Cook 15 minutes, or until broccoli is tender. Add salt, pepper, and cheese, then stir until cheese is melted.

Preparation time: 45 minutes

NUTRIENT INFORMATION

Servings per recipe: 4—Serving size: 1 1/4 cups

Protein 22 g, Carbohydrate 44 g, Fat 9 g, Saturated Fat 5 g, Cholesterol 30 mg, Sodium 691 mg, Dietary Fiber 1 g

Calories 345
From protein: 26%; From carbohydrate: 51%; From fat: 23%

Food Exchanges: 2 starch, 2 vegetable, 2 medium-fat meat

IRISH POTATO SOUP

from the White House Cookbook, 1894

Peel and boil eight medium-sized potatoes with a large onion sliced, some herbs, salt and pepper; press all through a colander; then thin it with rich milk and add a lump of butter, more seasoning, if necessary; let it heat well and serve hot.

FISH CHOWDER

from the White House Cookbook, 1894

Fry five or six slices of fat pork crisp in the bottom of the pot you are to make your chowder in; take them out and chop them into small pieces, put them back into the bottom of the pot with their own gravy. (This is much better than having the slices whole.)

Cut four pounds of fresh cod or sea bass into pieces two inches square, and lay enough of these on the pork to cover it. Follow with a layer of chopped onions, a little parsley, summer savory, and pepper, either black or cayenne. Then a layer of split Boston, or butter, or whole cream crackers, which have been soaked in warm water until moistened through, but not ready to break. Above this put a layer of pork and repeat the order given above—onions, seasoning (not too much), crackers, and pork, until your materials are exhausted. Let the topmost layer be buttered crackers well soaked. Pour in enough cold water to barely cover all. Cover the pot, stew gently for an hour, watching that the water does not sink too low. Should it leave the upper layer exposed, replenish cautiously from the boiling tea-kettle. When the chowder is thoroughly done, take out with a perforated skimmer and put into a tureen. Thicken the gravy with a tablespoonful of flour and about the same quantity of butter, boil up and pour over the chowder. Serve sliced lemon, pickles, and stewed tomatoes with it, that the guests may add if they like.

⁂FABULOUS FISH⁂
CHOWDER

"Chowder breathes reassurance. It steams consolation."
—Clementine Paddleford

1 medium onion, diced

2 tablespoons liquid Butter Buds®

3 1/2 cups potatoes, skinned, cubed, and cooked (about 3 large potatoes)

12 ounces evaporated skim milk

1 quart skim milk

3/4 pound cod or sea bass filet, cooked and cut in bite-size pieces

15 1/4-ounce can no-salt-added corn, drained

2 teaspoons salt

1/4 teaspoon cayenne pepper

1/8 teaspoon thyme

1 teaspoon chopped dried parsley

In a stock pot, sauté onion in Butter Buds until translucent. Add potatoes and milks. With a potato masher, mash about 1/2 of the potatoes to thicken the chowder. (May mash more potatoes if thicker chowder is desired.) Add fish, and corn. Stir in seasonings. Simmer uncovered for 45 minutes.

Preparation time: 1 hour 10 minutes (including cooking time for potatoes and fish)

NUTRIENT INFORMATION

Servings per recipe: 6—Serving size: 1 cup

*Protein 24 g, Carbohydrate 45 g, Fat 1 g, Saturated Fat <1 g,
Cholesterol 29 mg, Sodium 970 mg, Dietary Fiber 2 g*

*Calories 289
From protein: 35%; From carbohydrate: 62%; From fat: 3%*

Food Exchanges: 2 starch, 1 very lean meat, 1 skim milk

SQUIRREL SOUP

from the White House Cookbook, 1894

Wash and quarter three or four good-sized squirrels; put them on with a small tablespoonful of salt, directly after breakfast, in a gallon of cold water. Cover the pot close, and set it on the back part of the stove to simmer gently, not boil. Add vegetables just the same as you do in case of other meat soups in the summer season, but especially good will you find corn, Irish potatoes, tomatoes and Lima beans. Strain the soup through a coarse colander when the meat has boiled to shreds, so as to get rid of the squirrels' troublesome little bones. Then return to the pot, and after boiling a while longer, thicken with a piece of butter rubbed in flour. Celery and parsley leaves chopped up are also considered an improvement by many. Toast two slices of bread, cut them into dice one-half inch square, fry them in butter, put them into the bottom of your tureen, and then pour the soup boiling hot upon them. Very good.

ENTRÉES

TENDERLOIN OF BEEF

from the White House Cookbook, 1894

To serve tenderloin as directed below, the whole piece must be extracted before the hind-quarter of the animal is cut out. This must be particularly noted, because not commonly practiced, the tenderloin being usually left attached to the roasting pieces, in order to furnish a tidbit for a few. To dress it whole, proceed as follows: Washing the piece well, put it in an oven; add about a pint of water, and chop up a good handful of each of the following vegetables as an ingredient of the dish, viz., Irish potatoes, carrots, turnips and a large bunch of celery. They must be washed, peeled and chopped up raw, then added to the meat; blended with the juice, they form and flavor the gravy. Let the whole slowly simmer, and when nearly done, add a teaspoonful of pounded allspice. To give a richness to the gravy, put in a tablespoonful of butter. If the gravy should look too greasy, skim off some of the melted suet. Boil also a lean piece of beef, which, when perfectly done, chop fine, flavoring with a very small quantity of onion, besides pepper and salt to the taste. Make into small balls, wet then on the outside with eggs, roll in grated cracker or fine bread crumbs. Fry these force meat balls a light brown. When serving the dish, put these around the tenderloin, and pour over the whole the rich gravy. This dish is a very handsome one, and, altogether, fit for an epicurean palate. A sumptuous dish.

❊Blue Ribbon❊ Tenderloin Steaks
With Red Pepper Jelly

*This tasty dish is an adaptation of a winning recipe
from the 1993 National Beef Cook-Off. It's quick and tasty,
making it a sure winner for you too!*

4 (4-ounce) beef tenderloin steaks

1/2 teaspoon chili powder

1/2 teaspoon black pepper

1/8 teaspoon garlic salt

1/4 teaspoon oregano

1/4 teaspoon ground cumin

1 teaspoon olive oil

1/2 cup no-salt-added beef broth

1/4 cup red wine vinegar

2 tablespoons red jalapeno pepper jelly

Trim fat from steaks. Combine chili powder, pepper, garlic salt, oregano, and cumin and stir well. Rub chili powder mixture over both sides of steaks. Heat oil in a large nonstick skillet over medium-high heat until hot. Add steaks, and cook 4 minutes on each side or until desired degree of doneness. Remove steaks from skillet; set aside, and keep warm. Add broth, vinegar, and jelly to skillet and cook 5 minutes or until slightly thickened, stirring frequently. Spoon sauce over steaks.

Preparation time: 10 minutes—Cooking time: 15 minutes

Nutrient Information

Servings per recipe: 4—Serving size: 1 steak plus 1 tablespoon sauce

*Protein 23 g, Carbohydrate 11 g, Fat 6 g, Saturated Fat 2 g,
Cholesterol 65 mg, Sodium 133 mg, Dietary Fiber <1 g*

Calories 190
From protein: 48%; From carbohydrate: 23%; From fat: 28%

Food Exchanges: 3 lean meat, 2 vegetable

⊰MEAT AND POTATO PIE⊱

The original White House Cookbook proclaims this "a good, plain dish."
We think the centennial version is even better, and tastes far from plain!

1/2 pound ground round steak

1 cup chopped onion

1 large garlic clove, minced

1 teaspoon dried oregano

1 teaspoon dried basil

1/4 teaspoon dried thyme

1/4 teaspoon dried rosemary

3 cups quartered fresh mushrooms

1/4 cup whole wheat flour, dissolved in
1/4 cup dry white wine

14 1/2-ounce can diced tomatoes, undrained

1/8 teaspoon salt

1/8 teaspoon black pepper

1 cup no-salt-added French-style green beans

Cooking spray

1 1/2 pounds baking potatoes, peeled and cubed

1/3 cup skim milk

1/8 teaspoon salt

1/8 teaspoon black pepper

Cook meat, onion, and garlic in a large nonstick skillet over medium-high heat until browned, stirring to crumble. Drain well and return meat mixture to pan. Stir in oregano, basil, thyme and rosemary; cook over medium-high heat 1 minute. Add mushrooms; cook 2 minutes. Gradually add wine mixture, stirring constantly. Add tomatoes, 1/8 teaspoon salt, and 1/8 teaspoon pepper; cook 2 minutes or until thickened, stirring frequently. Remove from heat; stir in green beans. Spoon meat mixture into a 2-quart casserole coated with cooking spray; set aside.

Place potatoes in a large saucepan; cover with water and bring to a boil. Reduce heat, and cook 20 minutes or until very tender. Drain well, and

R O A S T   B E E F   P I E
W I T H   P O T A T O   C R U S T
from the White House Cookbook, 1894

When you have a cold roast of beef, cut off as much as will half fill a baking dish suited to the size of your family; put this sliced beef into a stewpan with any gravy that you may have also saved, a lump of butter, a bit of sliced onion and a seasoning of pepper and salt, with enough water to make plenty of gravy; thicken it, too, by dredging in a tablespoonful of flour; cover it up on the fire, where it may stew gently, but not be in danger of burning. Meanwhile there must be boiled a sufficient quantity of potatoes to fill up your baking dish, after the stewed meat has been transferred to it. The potatoes must be boiled done, mashed smooth, and beaten up with milk and butter, as if they were to be served alone, and placed in a thick layer on top of the meat. Brush it over with egg, place the dish in an oven, and let it remain there long enough to be brown. There should be a goodly quantity of gravy left with the beef, that the dish be not dry and tasteless.

return potatoes to pan. Add milk, salt, and pepper; beat at medium speed of a mixer until smooth. Spread mashed potatoes over meat mixture and bake at 375° for 30 minutes or until bubbly. Put casserole under the broiler for 3 minutes or until potatoes are browned.

Preparation time: 30 minutes—Cooking time: 1 hour and 5 minutes

N U T R I E N T   I N F O R M A T I O N

Servings per recipe: 4—Serving size: 2 cups

*Protein 19 g, Carbohydrate 57 g, Fat 9 g, Saturated Fat 3 g,
Cholesterol 35 mg, Sodium 528 mg, Dietary Fiber 2 g*

*Calories 385
From protein: 20%; From carbohydrate: 59%; From fat: 21%*

Food Exchanges: 3 starch, 1 medium-fat meat, 2 vegetable

BEEFSTEAK N^{O.} 1

from the White House Cookbook, 1894

The first consideration in broiling is to have a clear, glowing bed of coals. The steak should be about three-quarters of an inch in thickness, and should be pounded only in extreme cases, i.e., when it is cut too thick and is "stringy." Lay it on a buttered gridiron, turning it often, as it begins to drip, attempting nothing else while cooking it. Have everything else ready for the table; the potatoes and vegetables dished and in the warming closet. Do not season it until it is done, which will be in about ten to twelve minutes. Remove it to a warm platter, pepper and salt it on both sides and spread a liberal lump of butter over it. Serve at once while hot. No definite rule can be given as to the time of cooking steak—individual tastes differ so widely in regard to it, some only liking it when well done, others so rare that the blood runs out of it. The best pieces for broiling are the porter house and sirloin.

✠ALL-STAR SIRLOIN✠

Legend has it that King Charles II was so impressed with a platter of beef served at one of his feasts that he rose, touched his sword to the steaming platter and said, "Loin, I dub thee Knight— henceforth thou shall be known as Sir Loin."

1 1/2 teaspoons cracked black pepper

1 teaspoon thyme

1/4 teaspoon onion powder

1/4 teaspoon garlic powder

1/4 teaspoon cayenne pepper

1 pound lean, boneless sirloin steak

Cooking spray

Combine black pepper, thyme, onion powder, garlic powder, and cayenne pepper in a small bowl. Stir well. Trim fat from steak; press pepper mixture onto both sides of steak. Place steak on a rack coated with cooking spray; place rack in a shallow roasting pan. Broil 5 inches from heat 4 minutes on each side or to desired degree of doneness. Cut steak diagonally across the grain into 1/2-inch thick slices.

Preparation time: 10 minutes—Cooking time: 10 minutes

NUTRIENT INFORMATION

Servings per recipe: 4—Serving size: 3 ounces steak

Protein 22 g, Carbohydrate 1 g, Fat 5 g, Saturated Fat 2 g, Cholesterol 65 mg, Sodium 19 mg, Dietary Fiber <1 g

Calories 137
From protein: 64%; From carbohydrate: 3%; From fat: 33%

Food Exchanges: 3 very lean meat, 1 fat

⁑MICROWAVE SWEET⁑ AND SOUR "STIR-FRY"

Take advantage of modern microwave convenience by making this low-fat, high-flavor alternative to take-out Chinese food.

1 pound lean, boneless sirloin steak

8-ounce can unsweetened pineapple chunks, undrained

2 tablespoons low-sodium soy sauce

1 tablespoon white vinegar

1 clove garlic, minced

Cooking spray

1 cup diagonally sliced carrots

1 green pepper, julienne cut

1 red pepper, julienne cut

1/2 cup diced onion

1 cup canned whole baby corn, drained and chopped

1 tablespoon cornstarch

1/4 teaspoon brown sugar substitute

1/4 teaspoon ground ginger

1/8 teaspoon black pepper

8-ounce can sliced water chestnuts, drained

2 cups cooked brown rice

Trim fat from steak and slice across grain into 1/8 inch thick strips. Cut each strip in half lengthwise. Drain pineapple, reserving 1/4 cup plus 2 tablespoons juice. Combine 3 tablespoons of the remaining juice with soy sauce, cider vinegar, and garlic in a large zip-top heavy duty plastic bag. Add steak slices, seal bag and marinate in refrigerator 30 minutes. Remove steak from bag, reserving marinade; set both aside.

Combine remaining pineapple juice and carrots in a 3-quart casserole sprayed with cooking spray. Cover and microwave at high for 2 minutes. Stir in pineapple, peppers, onion, and corn. Cover and microwave at high for 3 minutes, stirring halfway through. Add steak to casserole; set aside.

S P I C E D B E E F

from the White House Cookbook, 1894

or a round of beef weighing twenty or twenty-four pounds, take one-quarter of a pound of saltpetre, one-quarter of a pound of coarse brown sugar, two pounds of salt, one ounce of cloves, one ounce of allspice and half an ounce of mace; pulverize these materials, mix them well together, and with them rub the beef thoroughly on every part; let the beef lie for eight or ten days in the pickle thus made, turning and rubbing it every day; then tie it around with a broad tape, to keep it in shape; make a coarse paste of flour and water, lay a little suet finely chopped over and under the beef, enclose the beef entirely in the paste and bake it six hours. When you take the beef from the oven, remove the paste, but do not remove the tape until you are ready to send it to the table. If you wish to eat the beef cold, keep it well covered that it may retain its moisture.

Combine cornstarch, brown sugar substitute, ginger and pepper in a bowl. Gradually add reserved marinade, stirring with a wire whisk until blended. Gently add water chestnuts. Add mixture to casserole. Microwave, uncovered, at high for 10 to 11 minutes or until thickened and bubbly, stirring every 3 minutes. Serve over rice.

Preparation time: 25 minutes—Marinating time: 30 minutes
Cooking time: 15 minutes

N U T R I E N T I N F O R M A T I O N

Servings per recipe: 4—Serving size: 1 1/2 cups beef mixture plus 1/2 cup rice

Protein 39 g, Carbohydrate 44 g, Fat 10 g, Saturated Fat 4 g,
Cholesterol 101 mg, Sodium 368 mg, Dietary Fiber 6 g

Calories 422
From protein: 37%; From carbohydrate: 42%; From fat: 21%

Food Exchanges: 2 starch, 5 very lean meat, 1 fruit, 1 fat

TO POT BEEF

from the White House Cookbook, 1894

The round is the best piece for potting, and you may use both the upper and under part. Take ten pounds of beef, remove all the fat, cut the lean into square pieces, two inches thick. Mix together three teaspoonfuls of salt, one of pepper, one of cloves, one of mace, one of cinnamon, one of allspice, one of thyme, and one of sweet basil. Put a layer of the pieces of beef into an earthen pot, sprinkle some of this spice mixture over this layer, add a piece of fat salt pork, cut as thin as possible, sprinkle a little of the spice mixture over the pork, make another layer of the beef with spices and pork, and so on, until the pot is filled. Pour over the whole three tablespoonfuls of Tarragon vinegar, or, if you prefer it, half a pint of Madeira wine; cover the pot with a paste made of flour and water, so that no steam can escape. Put the pot into an oven, moderately heated, and let it stand there eight hours; then set it away to use when wanted.

Beef cooked in this manner will keep good for a fortnight in moderate weather.

It is an excellent relish for breakfast, and may be eaten either warm or cold. When eaten warm, serve with slices of lemon.

☙ CROCKPOT ❧ BEEF ROAST

As President Harry S. Truman said, "If you can't stand the heat, get out of the kitchen." Take his advice and let your Crockpot do the work!

3-pound boneless pot roast

6 baking potatoes, peeled and cubed

1 medium onion, sliced

2 tablespoons whole wheat flour

1 tablespoon spicy brown mustard

1 tablespoon chili sauce

1 tablespoon Worcestershire sauce

1 teaspoon white vinegar

1 teaspoon sugar

1/2 teaspoon paprika

1/4 teaspoon black pepper

Trim excess fat from roast. Place potatoes and onion in bottom of Crockpot. Make a smooth paste of flour, mustard, chili sauce, Worcestershire sauce, vinegar, sugar, paprika, and pepper. Spread over top of roast. Place roast in Crockpot on top of potatoes and onion. (It may be necessary to cut roast in half to fit easily.) Cover and cook on LOW setting for 10-12 hours or on HIGH setting for 5-6 hours or until tender.

Preparation time: 15 minutes—Cooking time: 5-6 hours (HIGH) or 10-12 hours (LOW)

NUTRIENT INFORMATION

Servings per recipe: 8—Serving size: 1/8 recipe

Protein 31 g, Carbohydrate 43 g, Fat 16 g, Saturated Fat 6 g, Cholesterol 92 mg, Sodium 138 mg, Dietary Fiber 4 g

Calories 440
From protein: 28%; From carbohydrate: 39%; From fat: 33%

Food Exchanges: 3 starch, 3 lean meat, 1 fat

⊁Beef Steak⊱ Roll-Ups

"Beef is the soul of cooking."—Marie Antoine Careme

Cooking spray

1/2 cup shredded zucchini

1/4 cup chopped onion

1/4 cup chopped red pepper

1/4 cup chopped green pepper

1/2 teaspoon oregano

6 beef cube steaks

8-ounce can no-salt-added tomato sauce

2 tablespoons dry red wine

2 tablespoons chopped dried parsley

1/2 teaspoon dried Italian seasoning

1/4 teaspoon basil

1/4 teaspoon garlic powder

1 cup shredded fat-free mozzarella cheese

Coat a small nonstick skillet with cooking spray; place over medium heat until hot. Add zucchini, onion and peppers; sauté 2 to 3 minutes or until tender. Combine sautéed vegetables and oregano, stirring well. Place 2 tablespoons vegetable mixture on each cube steak, spreading to within 1/2 inch of edge. Roll up each steak jellyroll fashion; secure with a wooden pick. Wipe pan drippings from skillet with a paper towel; coat skillet with cooking spray. Place skillet over medium heat until hot. Add steak rolls; cook until browned on all sides.

Combine tomato sauce, wine, parsley, Italian seasoning, basil, and garlic powder; pour over steak rolls. Bring mixture to a boil. Reduce heat; cover and simmer 1 hour or until steak is tender. Sprinkle with cheese. Cover and heat just until cheese melts.

Preparation time: 20 minutes—Cooking time: 1 hours and 20 minutes

NUTRIENT INFORMATION

Servings per recipe: 6—Serving size: 1 roll-up

*Protein 42 g, Carbohydrate 6 g, Fat 10 g, Saturated Fat 4 g,
Cholesterol 101 mg, Sodium 224 mg, Dietary Fiber 1 g*

Calories 293
From protein: 57%; From carbohydrate: 8%; From fat: 31%

Food Exchanges: 6 very lean meat, 1 vegetable, 1 fat

SMOTHERED BEEFSTEAK
from the White House Cookbook, 1894

Take thin slices of steak from the upper part of the round or one large thin steak. Lay the meat out smoothly and wipe it dry. Prepare a dressing, using a cupful of fine bread crumbs, half a teaspoonful of salt, some pepper, a tablespoonful of butter, half a teaspoonful of sage, the same of powdered summer savory, and enough milk to moisten it all into a stiff mixture. Spread it over the meat, roll it up carefully, and tie with a string, securing the ends well. Now fry a few thin slices of salt pork in the bottom of a kettle or saucepan, and into the fat that has fried out of this pork, place this roll or rolls of beef, and brown it on all sides, turning it until a rich color all over; then add half a pint of water, and stew until tender. If the flavor of onion is liked, a slice may be chopped fine and added to the dressing. When cooked sufficiently, take out the meat, thicken the gravy and turn over it. To be carved cutting crosswise, in slices, through beef and stuffing.

POT ROAST (OLD STYLE)

from the White House Cookbook, 1894

*T*his is an old-fashioned dish, often cooked in our grandmothers' time. Take a piece of fresh beef weighing about five or six pounds. It must not be too fat. Wash it and put it into a pot with barely sufficient water to cover it. Set it over a slow fire, and after it has stewed an hour; salt and pepper it. Then stew it slowly until tender, adding a little onion if liked. Do not replenish the water at the last, but let all nearly boil away. When tender all through take the meat from the pot and pour gravy in a bowl. Put a large lump of butter in the bottom of the pot, then dredge the piece of meat with flour and return it to the pot to brown, turning it often to prevent its burning. Take the gravy that you have poured from the meat into the bowl and skim off all the fat; pour this gravy in with the meat and stir in a large spoonful of flour wet with a little water; let it boil up ten or fifteen minutes and pour into a gravy dish. Serve both hot: the meat on a platter. Some are very fond of this way of cooking a piece of beef which has been previously placed in spiced pickle for two or three days.

❧ PEPPERY POT ROAST ❧

Pot roast has been a family favorite for generations.
Our recipe is sure to continue the tradition of good taste.

4 1/2-pound lean, boneless rump roast

1/2 cup dry red wine

1/2 cup tomato sauce

1/2 cup white vinegar

2 green onions, minced

1 tablespoon spicy hot mustard

1 teaspoon thyme

1/2 teaspoon oregano

1/4 teaspoon cayenne pepper

1/2 teaspoon coarsely ground black pepper

1 bay leaf

Cooking spray

Trim excess fat from roast. Place roast in a large shallow dish. In a bowl, combine the next 9 ingredients, stirring with a wire whisk. Pour over roast. Add bay leaf. Cover and refrigerate 8 hours or overnight, turning roast occasionally.

Place roast, bay leaf, and marinade in a Dutch oven coated with cooking spray. Cover and bake at 350° for 2 1/2 hours or until meat is tender. Remove roast to serving platter. Skim fat from marinade, discard bay leaf, and serve marinade with roast.

Preparation time: 15 minutes—Marinating time: 8 hours
Cooking time: 2 hours and 30 minutes

NUTRIENT INFORMATION

Servings per recipe: 12—Serving size: 4 ounces roast (1/12 of recipe)

Protein 30 g, Carbohydrate 2 g, Fat 10 g, Saturated Fat 4 g,
Cholesterol 92 mg, Sodium 155 mg, Dietary Fiber <1 g

Calories 218
From protein: 55%; From carbohydrate: 4%; From fat: 41%

Food Exchanges: 4 lean meat

⚜COMPANY⚜ FLANK STEAK

The original White House Cookbook suggests that butchers frequently reserved the finest flank steak for themselves. We suggest that you share this delicious recipe with guests!

1 1/2-pound lean flank steak

3/4 cup red wine

1 teaspoon black pepper

1/2 teaspoon chopped dried parsley

1/4 teaspoon salt

1/4 teaspoon dried rosemary

1 medium onion, sliced and separated into rings

1/8 teaspoon garlic powder

Cooking spray

Trim fat from steak. Combine steak with next 7 ingredients in a large, zip-top heavy-duty plastic bag. Seal bag; marinate in refrigerator 8 hours, turning occasionally. Remove steak from marinade, reserving marinade. Place steak on a rack coated with cooking spray and place rack in broiler pan. Broil steak 3 inches from heat 7 minutes on each side or to desired degree of doneness. Cut steak diagonally across grain into thin slices. Keep warm. Pour reserved marinade into a large skillet. Bring to a boil and cook 5 minutes or until liquid evaporates, stirring occasionally. Serve remaining onions with steak.

Preparation time: 10 minutes—Marinating time: 8 hours
Cooking time: 20 minutes

NUTRIENT INFORMATION

Servings per recipe: 6—Serving size: 1/6 flank steak plus onions

Protein 28 g, Carbohydrate 3 g, Fat 9 g, Saturated Fat 4 g,
Cholesterol 47 mg, Sodium 149 mg, Dietary Fiber 1 g

Calories 205
From protein: 55%; From carbohydrate: 6%; From fat: 40%

Food Exchanges: 4 very lean meat, 1 vegetable, 1 fat

FLANK STEAK

from the White House Cookbook, 1894

*T*his is cut from the boneless part of the flank and is secreted between an outside and inside layer of creamy fat. There are two ways for broiling it. One is to slice diagonally across the grain; the other is to broil it whole. In either case, brush butter over it and proceed as in broiling other steaks. It is considered by butchers the finest steak, which they frequently reserve for themselves.

CURRY CHICKEN
from the White House Cookbook, 1894

*C*ut up a chicken weighing from a pound and a half to two pounds, as for fricassee, wash it well, and put it into a stewpan with sufficient water to cover it; boil it, closely covered, until tender; add a large teaspoonful of salt, and cook a few minutes longer; then remove from the fire, take out the chicken, pour the liquor into a bowl, and set it to one side. Now cut up into the stewpan two small onions, and fry them with a piece of butter as large as an egg; as soon as the onions are brown, skim them out and put in the chicken; fry for three or four minutes; next sprinkle over two teaspoonfuls of curry powder. Now pour over the liquor in which the chicken was stewed, stir all well together, and stew for five minutes longer, then stir into this a tablespoonful of sifted flour made thin with a little water; lastly, stir in a beaten yolk of egg, and it is done.

Serve with hot boiled rice laid around on the edge of a platter and the chicken curry in the centre.

This makes a handsome side dish, and a fine relish accompanying a full dinner of roast beef or any roast.

All first-class grocers and druggists keep this "India Curry Powder" put up in bottles. Beef, veal, mutton, duck, pigeons, partridges, rabbits or fresh fish may be substituted for the chicken, if preferred and sent to the table with or without a dish of rice.

❊ CAROL'S CURRIED ❊ CHICKEN CUTLETS

4 (4-ounce) skinless, boneless chicken breast halves

1 tablespoon curry powder, divided

2 tablespoons whole wheat flour

1/8 teaspoon salt

1/4 teaspoon cayenne pepper

Cooking spray

2 teaspoons canola oil

1 medium onion, sliced and separated into rings

1 clove garlic, minced

14 1/2-ounce can no-salt-added stewed tomatoes, undrained

1/3 cup golden raisins

1/4 cup fat-free sour cream

*P*lace each piece of chicken breast between 2 sheets of heavy-duty waxed paper; use a meat mallet or rolling pin to flatten to 1/4-inch thickness. Combine 1 teaspoon curry powder, whole wheat flour, salt, and cayenne pepper in a shallow dish; dredge chicken in flour mixture and set aside. Coat a nonstick skillet with cooking spray; add oil. Place over medium-high heat until hot. Add onion and garlic; sauté 3 minutes. Push onion and garlic to side of skillet. Add chicken and cook 2 minutes on each side or until browned. Add remaining curry powder, tomatoes, and raisins. Reduce heat to medium and cook chicken 2 minutes on each side. To serve, spoon sauce over chicken, and top with sour cream and garnish with parsley if desired.

Preparation time: 10 minutes—Cooking time: 15 minutes

NUTRIENT INFORMATION

Servings per recipe: 4—Serving size: 1 chicken breast,
2 tablespoons curry sauce, 1 tablespoon fat-free sour cream

Protein 31 g, Carbohydrate 44 g, Fat 6 g, Saturated Fat 1 g,
Cholesterol 69 mg, Sodium 789 mg, Dietary Fiber 4 g

Calories 354
From protein: 35%; From carbohydrate: 50%; From fat: 15%

Food Exchanges: 2 starch, 3 very lean meat, 1 fruit

☆ SPEEDY GRILLED ☆ CHICKEN

Only a handful of ingredients, but a lot of good taste in this quick grilled chicken dish! Serve with our Southwestern Corn on the Cob for your next cook-out.

1 teaspoon parsley

1/2 teaspoon basil

1/2 teaspoon thyme

1/2 teaspoon oregano

1/8 teaspoon garlic salt

6 (4-ounce) boneless, skinless chicken breast halves

1 tablespoon canola oil

Juice of 1 lemon

Cooking spray

Combine parsley, basil, thyme, oregano, and garlic salt in a small bowl; set aside. Trim excess fat from chicken. Rinse chicken and pat dry. Place each chicken breast half between 2 sheets of heavy duty plastic wrap and flatten to 1/4 inch thickness using a meat mallet or rolling pin. Brush surface of chicken with olive oil; sprinkle with lemon juice and reserved herbs. Coat grill with cooking spray, taking care to keep cooking spray away from heat. Grill chicken 6 inches over medium coals 10 minutes or until chicken is tender, turning once.

Preparation time: 20 minutes—Cooking time: 10 minutes

NUTRIENT INFORMATION:

Servings per recipe: 6—Serving size: 1 chicken breast half

Protein 25 g, Carbohydrate 1 g, Fat 5 g, Saturated Fat 1 g, Cholesterol 69 mg, Sodium 62 mg, Dietary Fiber <1 g

Calories 149
From protein: 67%; From carbohydrate: 3%; From fat: 30%

Food Exchanges: 4 very lean meat

FRICASSEE CHICKEN
from the White House Cookbook, 1894

Cut up two young chickens; put them in a stewpan with just enough cold water to cover them. Cover closely and let them heat very slowly; then stew them over an hour, or until tender. If they are old chickens, they will require long, slow boiling, often from three to four hours. When tender, season with salt and pepper, a piece of butter as large as an egg, and a little celery, if liked. Stir up two table-spoonfuls of flour in a little water or milk and add to the stew, also two well-beaten yolks of eggs; let all boil up one minute; arrange the chicken on a warm platter, pour some of the gravy over it and send the rest to the table in a boat. The egg should be added to a little of the cooled gravy before putting with the hot gravy.

FRIED CHICKEN

from the White House Cookbook, 1894

Wash and cut up a young chicken, wipe it dry, season with salt and pepper, dredge it with flour, or dip each piece in beaten egg and then in cracker crumbs. Have in a frying pan one ounce each of butter and sweet lard made boiling hot. Lay in the chicken and fry brown on both sides. Take up, drain it and set aside in a covered dish. Stir into the gravy left, if not too much, a large tablespoonful of flour; make it smooth; add a cup of cream or milk; season with salt and pepper; boil up and pour over the chicken. Some like chopped parsley added to the gravy. Serve hot.

If the chicken is old, put into a stewpan with a little water and simmer gently till tender; season with salt and pepper; dip in flour or cracker crumb and egg, and fry as above. Use the broth the chicken was cooked in to make the gravy, instead of the cream or milk, or use an equal quantity of both.

❧ SKINNY SOUTHERN ❧ "FRIED" CHICKEN

"Only a Southerner knows how to fry a chicken—period!" —Anonymous

3/4 cup fine, dry breadcrumbs

1 tablespoon grated Parmesan cheese

1/2 teaspoon black pepper

1/4 teaspoon garlic salt

1/4 teaspoon basil

1/4 teaspoon oregano

1/4 teaspoon paprika

4 (4-ounce) skinless, boneless chicken breast halves

3 tablespoons evaporated skim milk

Cooking spray

1 tablespoon olive oil

Combine breadcrumbs, cheese, pepper, garlic salt, basil, oregano, and paprika in a shallow dish. Dip chicken in evaporated milk, then coat with crumb mixture. Place in a shallow roasting pan coated with cooking spray. Bake at 400° for 30 minutes; brush with olive oil and bake 10 minutes longer.

Preparation time: 25 minutes—Cooking time: 40 minutes

NUTRIENT INFORMATION

Servings per recipe: 4—Serving size: 1 chicken breast half

Protein 28 g, Carbohydrate 14 g, Fat 6 g, Saturated Fat 1 g, Cholesterol 70 mg, Sodium 276 mg, Dietary Fiber <1 g

Calories 222
From protein: 50%; From carbohydrate: 25%; From fat: 24%

Food Exchanges: 1 starch, 3 very lean meat, 1 fat

❊Parisian Chicken❊ Roll-Ups

"A chicken in every pot."—President Herbert Hoover

Fresh herbs and spices enhance this dish, adding so much flavor you won't realize that a considerable amount of the calories, fat, and sodium have vanished!

1/4 cup loosely packed fresh parsley

1 tablespoon fresh tarragon

1 tablespoon fresh chervil

1 tablespoon fresh thyme leaves

1/2 teaspoon coarsely ground black pepper

3 slices whole wheat bread, toasted

1 egg white, lightly beaten

1 tablespoon water

6 (4-ounce) skinless, boneless chicken breast halves

3 slices 97% fat-free ham, halved

3 slices reduced-fat Swiss cheese, halved

Cooking spray

Combine parsley, tarragon, chervil, thyme, pepper, and bread in a food processor and process until crumbs are fine; place crumbs in a shallow dish and set aside. Combine egg white and water in a shallow bowl; stir well and set aside.

Place each chicken breast half between 2 sheets of heavy-duty plastic wrap and flatten to 1/4 inch thickness using a meat mallet or rolling pin. Top each piece with 1/2 slice of ham and 1/2 slice of cheese. Roll up jelly-roll fashion. Tuck in sides; secure each roll with wooden pick. Dip each roll in egg white mixture; dredge in breadcrumb mixture. Place rolls, seam sides down, on a jelly-roll pan coated with cooking spray. Bake at 350° for 30 minutes or until done. Discard wooden picks. Cut each roll into thin slices. Garnish with fresh basil sprigs, if desired.

Preparation time: 30 minutes—Cooking time: 30 minutes

NUTRIENT INFORMATION

Servings per recipe: 6—Serving size: 1 chicken roll

Protein 32 g, Carbohydrate 7 g, Fat 6 g, Saturated Fat 2 g,
Cholesterol 79 mg, Sodium 220 mg, Dietary Fiber 1 g

Calories 210
From protein: 61%; Carbohydrate: 13%; From fat: 26%

Food Exchanges: 4 very lean meat, 1 vegetable, 1 fat

CHICKEN ROLY-POLY

from the White House Cookbook, 1894

One quart of flour, two teaspoonfuls of cream of tartar mixed with the flour, one teaspoonful of soda dissolved in a teacupful of milk; a teaspoonful of salt; do not use shortening of any kind, but roll out the mixture half an inch thick, and on it lay minced chicken, veal or mutton. The meat must be seasoned with pepper and salt and be free from gristle. Roll the crust over and over, and put it on a buttered plate and place in a steamer for half an hour. Serve for breakfast or lunch, giving a slice to each person with gravy served with it.

❧ CILANTRO CHICKEN ❧ WITH BLACK BEAN SALSA

"Poultry is for the cook what canvas is for the painter."
—Jean Anthelme Brillat-Savarin

2 tablespoons olive oil

1/2 teaspoon chili powder

1/4 teaspoon garlic powder

1/4 teaspoon cilantro

Juice of 1 lime

4 (4-ounce) skinless, boneless chicken breast halves

1/8 teaspoon salt

1/4 teaspoon black pepper

1/4 cup sliced green onions

15-ounce can no-salt-added black beans, rinsed and drained

8-ounce can no-salt-added white shoepeg corn, rinsed and drained

4 1/2-ounce can chopped green chilies, undrained

2-ounce jar diced pimento, drained

Cooking spray

Mix olive oil, chili powder, garlic powder, cilantro, and lime juice in a small bowl. Place chicken in a shallow dish; sprinkle with salt and pepper on both sides and drizzle with 1 tablespoon seasoned oil. Cover and marinate in refrigerator 20 minutes. Combine the remaining seasoned oil, green onions, beans, corn, chilies, and pimento in a medium bowl; stir well. Place chicken on a broiler pan coated with cooking spray and broil 6 minutes on each side or until done. Cut chicken into thin slices. Spoon bean mixture onto individual plates and top with sliced chicken. Garnish with cilantro sprigs if desired.

Preparation time: 15 minutes—Marinating time: 20 minutes
Cooking time: 12 minutes

NUTRIENT INFORMATION

Servings per recipe: 4—Serving size: 1 chicken breast half with 2/3 cup salsa

Protein 36 g, Carbohydrate 36 g, Fat 9 g, Saturated Fat 2 g,
Cholesterol 69 mg, Sodium 369 mg, Dietary Fiber 6 g

Calories 333
From protein: 43%; From carbohydrate: 43%; Fat: 14%

Food Exchanges: 1 starch, 5 very lean meat, 2 vegetable, 1 fat

STEAMED CHICKEN
from the White House Cookbook, 1894

Rub the chicken on the inside with pepper and half a teaspoonful of salt; place in a steamer in a kettle that will keep it as near the water as possible, cover and steam an hour and a half; when done, keep hot while dressing is prepared, then cut up, arrange on the platter, and serve with the dressing over it.

The dressing is made as follows: Boil one pint of gravy from the kettle without the fat, add cayenne pepper and half a teaspoonful of salt; stir a tablespoonful of flour into a quarter of a pint of cream until smooth and add to the gravy. Cornstarch may be used instead of the flour, and some cooks add nutmeg or celery salt.

❧Good-for-You❧ Chicken Pot Pie

"There is nothing better on a cold wintry day than a properly made pot pie."
—*Craig Claiborne*

Low-Fat Pie Crust:

1 cup plus 2 tablespoons whole wheat flour

1/4 teaspoon salt

5 tablespoons cold water

2 1/2 tablespoons corn oil

Cooking spray

Mix flour and salt thoroughly. Mix 1/4 cup of the flour and salt mixture with the cold water to make a paste; set aside. Using a fork, lightly mix oil with remaining flour and salt mixture until mixture is crumbly. Stir flour and salt paste into flour and oil mixture to form a ball. Roll dough between 2 sheets of wax paper sprayed with cooking spray until the dough is at least 1 inch wider all around than the pie pan. Set aside.

Filling:

2 (10 3/4-ounce) cans reduced-fat-and-sodium cream of chicken soup

15-ounce can no-salt-added mixed vegetables, drained

1 1/2 cups cooked, diced chicken

1/2 cup skim milk

1 teaspoon savory

1/2 teaspoon thyme

1/8 teaspoon black pepper

Cooking spray

Combine cream of chicken soup, mixed vegetables, chicken, skim milk, savory, thyme, and black pepper in a large bowl. Pour into 9" pie plate coated with cooking spray. Cover with crust. Crimp edge to pie plate. Slit crust to vent. Bake at 375° for 40 minutes. Cool 10 minutes before serving.

Preparation time: 25 minutes—Cooking time: 40 minutes
Cooling time: 10 minutes

NUTRIENT INFORMATION

Servings per recipe: 6—Serving size: 1/6 pie

Protein 22 g, Carbohydrate 45 g, Fat 12 g, Saturated Fat 1 g,
Cholesterol 39 mg, Sodium 578 mg, Dietary Fiber 6 g

Calories 376
From protein: 23%; From carbohydrate: 48%; From fat: 29%

Food Exchanges: 2 starch, 2 very lean meat, 2 vegetable, 1 fat

CHICKEN POT PIE

from the White House Cookbook, 1894

Cut and joint a large chicken, cover with cold water, and let it boil gently until tender. Season with salt and pepper, and thicken the gravy with two tablespoonfuls of flour, mixed smooth with a piece of butter the size of an egg. Have ready nice light bread-dough, cut with the top of a wineglass about a half an inch thick; let them stand half an hour and rise, then drop these into the boiling gravy. Put the cover on the pot closely, wrap a cloth around it, in order that no steam shall escape; and by no means allow the pot to cease boiling. Boil three-quarters of an hour.

⊰Cheese-Stuffed⊱ Italian Chicken

This dish is special enough to serve for guests. Substituting boneless chicken breast halves for cannelloni noodles gives it a unique twist!

Cooking spray

1 cup thinly sliced celery

1/2 cup sliced fresh mushrooms

1/4 cup shredded carrots

1 small onion, thinly sliced

1 clove garlic, minced

1 1/2 teaspoons oregano, divided

8-ounce can no-salt-added tomato sauce

7 1/2-ounce can no-salt-added diced tomatoes, undrained

1 teaspoon sugar

1/2 cup fat-free cottage cheese

2 tablespoons grated Parmesan cheese

1 tablespoon chopped fresh chives

1/8 teaspoon black pepper

6 (4-ounce) boneless, skinless chicken breast halves

1/4 cup finely shredded, fat-free mozzarella cheese

Coat a medium saucepan with cooking spray; place over medium-high heat until hot. Add celery, mushrooms, carrots, onion, and garlic; sauté until tender. Add 1 teaspoon oregano, tomato sauce, diced tomatoes, and sugar. Bring to a boil. Reduce heat and cook, uncovered, 20 minutes or until reduced to about 2 cups. Set mixture aside.

Combine remaining 1/2 teaspoon oregano, cottage cheese, Parmesan cheese, chives, and pepper. Set aside.

Place each chicken breast half between 2 sheets of heavy-duty plastic wrap and flatten to 1/4 inch thickness, using a meat mallet or rolling pin. Spread

FRIED CHICKEN À LA ITALIENNE
from the White House Cookbook, 1894

*M*ake common batter; mix into it a cupful of chopped tomatoes, one onion chopped, some minced parsley, salt and pepper. Cut up young, tender chickens, dry them well and dip each piece in the batter; then fry brown in plenty of butter in a thick-bottomed frying pan. Serve with tomato sauce.

1 1/2 tablespoons cheese mixture over each piece of chicken; roll up lengthwise. Place 1 chicken roll, seam side down, into each of 6 individual casserole dishes coated with cooking spray. Spoon 1/3 cup tomato mixture over each roll.

Cover and bake at 375° for 45 minutes or until done. Uncover; sprinkle each roll with 2 teaspoons mozzarella cheese. Bake an additional 3 minutes or until cheese melts.

Preparation time: 35 minutes—Cooking time: 1 hour and 15 minutes

NUTRIENT INFORMATION

Servings per recipe: 6—Serving size: 1 stuffed chicken breast

Protein 30 g, Carbohydrate 10 g, Fat 4 g, Saturated Fat 1 g, Cholesterol 72 mg, Sodium 245 mg, Dietary Fiber 2 g

Calories 196
From protein: 61%; From carbohydrate: 20%; From fat: 18%

Food Exchanges: 4 very lean meat, 2 vegetable

❊Lightened-Up❊ Chicken Croquettes

Chicken croquettes are traditionally made by mixing chopped chicken with flour and spices, shaping it into balls, rolling the balls in bread crumbs, dipping them in beaten eggs, rolling them in crumbs again and finally, frying them in deep fat. Our recipe lightens up the calories, fat, and work!

2 tablespoons reduced-calorie margarine

2 tablespoons whole wheat flour

1 cup skim milk

1 teaspoon Worcestershire sauce

1 teaspoon parsley

1/4 teaspoon salt

1/8 teaspoon cayenne pepper

2 cups cooked chicken breast, shredded

2/3 cup fine, dry herbed bread crumbs

1/2 cup liquid egg substitute

Cooking spray

Melt margarine over low heat; stir in flour until smooth. Add milk gradually and whisk until smooth; then stir in Worcestershire sauce, parsley, salt, pepper, and chicken. Cool in refrigerator for 1 hour. When cold, form mixture into 8 balls using 1/3 cup mixture per ball. Roll each ball in bread crumbs, then in slightly beaten egg substitute and again in bread crumbs. Place on cookie sheet coated with cooking spray. Bake at 375° for 25 to 30 minutes, or until light golden brown.

Preparation time: 10 minutes—Cooling time: 1 hour
Cooking time: 25 minutes

NUTRIENT INFORMATION

Servings per recipe: 4—Serving size: 2 croquettes

*Protein 17 g, Carbohydrate 9 g, Fat 4 g, Saturated Fat 1 g,
Cholesterol 35 mg, Sodium 239 mg, Dietary Fiber <1 g*

*Calories 140
From protein: 49%; From carbohydrate: 26%; From fat: 26%*

Food Exchanges: 1 starch, 2 very lean meat

RISSOLES OF CHICKEN

from the White House Cookbook, 1894

ince up finely the remains of a cold chicken together with half the quantity of lean, cold ham. Mix them well, adding enough white sauce to moisten them. Now have light paste rolled out until about a quarter of an inch or a little more in thickness. Cut the paste into pieces, one inch by two in size, and lay a little of the mixture upon the centres of half of the pieces and cover them with the other halves, pressing the edges neatly together and forming them into little rolls. Have your frying pan ready with plenty of boiling hot lard, or other frying medium, and fry until they become a golden-brown color. A minute or two will be sufficient for this. Then drain them well and serve immediately on a napkin.

⚜ QUICK CHICKEN ⚜ PATTIES

Which came first—the chicken or the egg? Both ingredients contribute to this delicious, quick alternative to ground beef patties.

1 pound freshly ground raw chicken breast

1 small onion, chopped

1/4 cup fine, dry herbed breadcrumbs

2 1/2 tablespoons parsley

1/2 teaspoon thyme

1/4 teaspoon black pepper

1/8 teaspoon cayenne pepper

1/8 teaspoon salt

1 egg white

1/4 cup whole wheat flour

Cooking spray

1 teaspoon canola oil

1/2 cup dry white wine

1/2 teaspoon savory

Combine chicken, onion, breadcrumbs, parsley, thyme, peppers, salt, and egg white in a bowl; stir well. Divide mixture into 4 equal portions, shaping each into a 3/4-inch thick patty. Place flour in a shallow dish; dredge patties in flour and set aside.

Coat a nonstick skillet with cooking spray; add oil and place over medium heat until hot. Add patties; cook 3 minutes on each side. Cover and cook an additional 3 minutes or until done. Remove from skillet; set aside and keep warm.

Add wine and tarragon to skillet; scrape bottom of skillet with a wooden spoon to loosen browned bits. Cook 1 minute or until wine is reduced by half. Spoon sauce over patties.

Preparation time: 15 minutes—Cooking time: 15 minutes

NUTRIENT INFORMATION

Servings per recipe: 4—Serving size: 1 chicken patty plus 1 tablespoon sauce

Protein 28 g, Carbohydrate 13 g, Fat 5 g, Saturated Fat 1 g,
Cholesterol 69 mg, Sodium 188 mg, Dietary Fiber 1 g

Calories 227
From protein: 49%; From carbohydrate: 23%; From fat: 20%; From alcohol: 8%

Food Exchanges: 1 starch, 4 very lean meat

CHICKEN PATTIES
from the White House Cookbook, 1894

Mince up fine cold chicken, either roasted or boiled. Season it with pepper and salt, and a little minced parsley, and onion. Moisten it with chicken gravy or cream sauce, fill scalloped shells that are lined with pastry with the mixture, and sprinkle bread crumbs over the tops. Put two or three tiny pieces of butter over each, and bake brown in a hot oven.

SCALLOPED CHICKEN

from the White House Cookbook, 1894

*D*ivide a fowl into joint and boil till the meat leaves the bone readily. Take out the bones and chop the meat as small as dice. Thicken the water in which the fowl was boiled with flour and season to taste with butter and salt. Fill a deep dish with alternate layers of bread crumbs and chicken and slices of cooked potatoes, having crumbs on top. Put the gravy over the top and add a few bits of butter and bake till nicely browned. There should be gravy enough to moisten the dish. Serve with a garnish of parsley. Tiny new potatoes are nice in place of sliced ones when in season.

❧TEX-MEX CHICKEN❧ POTATO BAKE

This well-seasoned recipe accents an interesting idea—using a shredded baking potato to provide a fat-free coating for chicken!

1 large baking potato, peeled and shredded

1/4 cup nonfat buttermilk

1 teaspoon chili powder

1 teaspoon oregano

1/2 teaspoon cumin

1/2 teaspoon cilantro

1/4 teaspoon cayenne pepper

4 (6-ounce) boneless, skinless chicken breast halves

Cooking spray

1 teaspoon olive oil

Place shredded potato in ice water; let stand 5 minutes. Combine buttermilk, chili powder, oregano, cumin, cilantro, and cayenne pepper; brush over both sides of chicken. Line a cookie sheet with aluminum foil; coat foil with cooking spray. Place chicken in prepared pan.

Drain shredded potato and pat dry with paper towels. Place in a small bowl; add oil and toss gently. Spoon 1/3 cup potato mixture over each chicken breast half; spread evenly over top of chicken. Bake at 425° for 35 minutes or until chicken is done and potato is golden.

Preparation time: 15 minutes—Cooking time: 35 minutes

NUTRIENT INFORMATION

Servings per recipe: 4—Serving size: 1 chicken breast half

Protein 40 g, Carbohydrate 14 g, Fat 6 g, Saturated Fat 1 g, Cholesterol 104 mg, Sodium 115 mg, Dietary Fiber 2 g

Calories 270
From protein: 59%; From carbohydrate: 21%; From fat: 20%

Food Exchanges: 1 starch, 5 very lean meat

❧ KENTUCKY DERBY ❧ TURKEY HASH

In the 19th century, hash was often used as the centerpiece of a hearty Southern plantation breakfast. Our version has been lightened up to suit modern tastes.

Cooking spray

1 cup sliced fresh mushrooms

2 tablespoons chopped onion

2 tablespoons chopped green pepper

2 tablespoons chopped red pepper

3 tablespoons reduced-calorie margarine

5 tablespoons whole wheat flour

1 1/2 teaspoons low-sodium chicken bouillon granules

1 1/2 cups skim milk

1 1/2 cups water

1/2 teaspoon black pepper

1/4 teaspoon paprika

5 cups boneless, skinless turkey breast, cooked and chopped

Parsley sprigs

Coat a large nonstick skillet with cooking spray. Place over medium heat until hot. Add mushrooms, onion, and peppers. Cook until vegetables are tender. Remove vegetables from skillet and set aside. Melt margarine in skillet over low heat. Add flour and bouillon granules, stirring until smooth. Cook 1 minute, stirring constantly (mixture will be dry). Gradually add milk and water; cook over medium heat, stirring constantly with a wire whisk, until smooth and thickened. Stir in pepper, paprika, turkey, and reserved vegetables; heat thoroughly. Garnish with parsley sprigs.

Preparation time: 25 minutes—Cooking time: 45 minutes

N U T R I E N T   I N F O R M A T I O N

Servings per recipe: 8—Serving size: 1 cup

Protein 24 g, Carbohydrate 7 g, Fat 3 g, Saturated Fat 1 g,
Cholesterol 60 mg, Sodium 112 mg, Dietary Fiber <1 g

Calories 151
From protein: 64%; From carbohydrate: 19%; From fat: 18%

Food Exchanges: 3 very lean meat, 1 vegetable

T U R K E Y   H A S H E D
from the White House Cookbook, 1894

Cut the remnants of turkey from a previous dinner into pieces of equal size. Boil the bones in a quart of water, until the quart is reduced to a pint; then take out the bones, and to the liquor in which they were boiled add turkey gravy, if you have any, or white stock, or a small piece of butter with salt and pepper; let the liquor thus prepared boil up once; then put in the pieces of turkey, dredge in a little flour, give it one boil-up and serve in a hot dish.

CRUNCHY TURKEY CASSEROLE

James Dent defined eternity as "two people and a roast turkey."
However, we think this scrumptious casserole will make you glad
you have Thanksgiving leftovers!

10-ounce package frozen peas, thawed and drained

2 cups boneless, skinless turkey, cooked and cubed

3/4 cup reduced-fat, shredded sharp cheddar cheese, divided

1 cup fresh mushrooms, sliced

1/3 cup reduced-calorie mayonnaise

1 teaspoon Dijon mustard

1/8 teaspoon paprika

1/8 teaspoon salt

1/8 teaspoon black pepper

8-ounce can sliced water chestnuts, drained

2 tablespoons diced pimento

Cooking spray

Combine peas, turkey, 1/2 cup cheese, and mushrooms in a medium bowl; set aside. Combine mayonnaise, mustard, paprika, salt, and pepper in a small bowl. Add to turkey mixture, tossing well. Stir in water chestnuts and pimento. Spoon into a 2-quart casserole coated with cooking spray; sprinkle with remaining cheese. Bake at 350° for 30 minutes or until bubbly.

Preparation time: 15 minutes—Cooking time: 30 minutes

N U T R I E N T   I N F O R M A T I O N

Servings per recipe: 6—Serving size: 1 cup

*Protein 15 g, Carbohydrate 14 g, Fat 2 g, Saturated Fat 1 g,
Cholesterol 30 mg, Sodium 364 mg, Dietary Fiber 3 g*

Calories 134
From protein: 45%; From carbohydrate: 42%; From fat: 13%

Food Exchanges: 1 starch, 2 very lean meat

T U R K E Y   S C A L L O P

from the White House Cookbook, 1894

*P*ick the meat from the bones of cold turkey and chop
it fine. Put a layer of bread crumbs on the bottom of a
buttered dish, moisten them with a little milk; then put in a layer
of turkey with some of the filling, and cut small pieces of butter over
the top; sprinkle with pepper and salt; then another layer of bread
crumbs, and so on until the dish is nearly full; add a little hot water
to the gravy left from the turkey and pour over it; then take two eggs,
two tablespoonfuls of milk, one of melted butter, a little salt and
cracker crumbs as much as will make it thick enough to spread
on with a knife; put bits of butter over it, and cover with a plate.
Bake three-quarters of an hour. Ten minutes before serving,
remove the plate and let it brown.

BRAISED DUCK

from the White House Cookbook, 1894

*P*repare a pair of fine young ducks, the same as for roasting, place them in a stewpan together with two or three slices of bacon, a carrot, an onion stuck with two cloves, and a little thyme and parsley. Season with pepper, and cover the whole with a broth, adding to the broth a gill of white wine. Place the pan over a gentle fire and allow the ducks to simmer until done, basting them frequently. When done, remove them from the pan, and place them where they will keep hot. A turnip should then be cut up and fried in some butter. When nicely browned, drain the pieces and cook them until tender in the liquor in which the ducks were braised. Now strain and thicken the gravy, and after dishing up the ducks, pour it over them, garnishing with the pieces of turnip.

⊰DUCKLING BREASTS⊱ ITALIANO

Duck is a form of poultry. Nutritionally, it is similar to chicken or turkey, and most often cooked in the same way. Although the vast majority of duck is produced in China, it is enjoying a resurgence of popularity in the United States.

4 (4-ounce) skinless, boneless duckling breasts

1/4 teaspoon black pepper

1 tablespoon dried oregano

2 teaspoons dried basil

Cooking spray

1/4 cup Dijon mustard

1/3 cup grated, fat free Parmesan cheese

1/3 cup sherry

Wash duckling breasts and pat dry. Sprinkle both sides with pepper, oregano, and basil. Place breasts in a large nonstick skillet coated with cooking spray. Cook breasts over medium-high heat for 10 minutes on each side. Remove breasts from skillet and place in baking dish coated with cooking spray. Mix mustard, cheese, and sherry; pour over duckling breasts. Bake at 350° for 25 minutes or until tender. Garnish with parsley before serving if desired.

Preparation time: 10 minutes—Cooking time: 45 minutes

NUTRIENT INFORMATION

Servings per recipe: 4—Serving size: 1 breast with 1/4 cup sauce

*Protein 37 g, Carbohydrate 6 g, Fat 8 g, Saturated Fat 2 g,
Cholesterol 0, Sodium 533 mg, Dietary Fiber <1 g*

Calories 255
From protein: 58%; From carbohydrate: 9%; From fat: 28%; From alcohol: 4%

Food Exchanges: 5 very lean meat, 1 vegetable, 1 fat

⊰FAVORITE⊱ LAMB CHOPS

Since Biblical times, lamb meat has been noted for its delicate flavor and tenderness. This spicy dish is certain to become a family favorite for you too!

8 (4-ounce) lean lamb loin chops

Cooking spray

1 1/4 cup orange juice, divided

2 tablespoons canned chopped green chilies, drained

1/4 teaspoon ground cumin

1/4 teaspoon cayenne pepper

1 tablespoon plus 2 teaspoons cornstarch

2/3 cup diced, unpeeled tomato

1/2 cup diced green pepper

2/3 cup mandarin orange sections

Trim fat from chops. Coat a nonstick skillet with cooking spray. Place over medium-high heat until hot. Add chops; cook 2 minutes on each side. Remove chops from skillet, wipe drippings from the skillet with a paper towel and return chops to skillet.

Combine 1 cup orange juice, chilies, cumin, and cayenne pepper. Add to skillet. Cook over medium heat 5 minutes. Remove chops from skillet; keep warm. Combine remaining 1/4 cup orange juice and cornstarch in a bowl. Stir well. Add cornstarch mixture, tomato, green pepper, and mandarin oranges to skillet. Bring to a boil and cook 1 minute or until thickened. Spoon sauce over chops.

Preparation time: 10 minutes—Cooking time: 15 minutes

NUTRIENT INFORMATION

Servings per recipe: 4—Serving size: 2 lamb chops plus 1/2 cup sauce

*Protein 46 g, Carbohydrate 16 g, Fat 17 g, Saturated Fat 6 g,
Cholesterol 147 mg, Sodium 207 mg, Dietary Fiber 1 g*

*Calories 401
From protein: 46%; From carbohydrate: 16%; From fat: 38%*

Food Exchanges: 6 lean meat, 1 fruit

ROAST QUARTER OF LAMB

from the White House Cookbook, 1894

Procure a nice hind-quarter; remove some of the fat that is around the kidney; skewer the lower joint up to the fillet; place it in a moderate oven; let it heat through slowly; then dredge it with salt and flour; quicken the fire; put half a pint of water into the dripping-pan, with a teaspoonful of salt. With this liquor, baste the meat occasionally; serve with lettuce, green peas and mint sauce.

A quarter of lamb weighing seven or eight pounds
will require two hours to roast.

A breast of lamb roasted is very sweet and is considered by many as preferable to hind-quarter. It requires nearly as long a time to roast as the quarter, and should be served in the same manner.

Make the gravy from the drippings, thickened with flour.

The mint sauce is made as follows: Take fresh, young spearmint leaves stripped from stems; wash and drain them or dry on a cloth, chop very fine; put in a gravy tureen, and to three tablespoonfuls of mint add two of finely powdered cut-loaf sugar; mix, and let it stand a few minutes, then pour over it six tablespoonfuls good cider or white-wine vinegar. The sauce should be made some time before dinner, so that the flavor of the mint may be well extracted.

PORK TENDERLOINS

from the White House Cookbook, 1894

*T*he tenderloins are unlike any other part of the pork in flavor. They may be either fried or broiled; the latter being drier, require to be well-buttered before serving, which should be done on a hot platter before the butter becomes oily. Fry them in a little lard, turning them to have them cooked through; when done, remove, and keep hot while making a gravy by dredging a little flour into the hot fat; if not enough, add a little butter or lard, stir until browned and add a little milk or cream; stir briskly, and pour over the dish. A little Worcestershire sauce may be added to the gravy if desired.

❊PRESIDENTIAL PORK❊ LOIN PICANTE

This spicy-sweet pork recipe is quick and tasty!

1 tablespoon chili powder

1 teaspoon cumin

1/4 teaspoon cayenne pepper

1/4 teaspoon garlic powder

1/4 teaspoon onion powder

1 pound boneless pork loin, cubed

Cooking spray

2 teaspoons olive oil

8-ounce jar mild, thick and chunky salsa

4 tablespoons peach preserves

Place chili powder, cumin, cayenne pepper, garlic powder, and onion powder in a large zip-top heavy-duty plastic bag. Add pork cubes; close top and shake to coat pork with seasonings. Coat large nonstick skillet with cooking spray; add olive oil and heat until medium-hot. Add pork cubes and brown. Add salsa and peach preserves to skillet; stir to mix well, cover and lower heat. Simmer gently for 15 minutes.

Preparation time: 15 minutes—Cooking time: 30 minutes

NUTRIENT INFORMATION

Servings per recipe. 4—Serving size: 1/4 recipe

Protein 26 g, Carbohydrate 18 g, Fat 5 g, Saturated Fat 2 g, Cholesterol 60 mg, Sodium 550 mg, Dietary Fiber 2 g

Calories 221
From protein: 47%; From carbohydrate: 33%; From fat: 20%

Food Exchanges: 4 very lean meat, 1 fruit

PORK CHOPS AND FRIED APPLES

from the White House Cookbook, 1894

Season the chops with salt and pepper and a little powdered sage; dip them into bread crumbs. Fry about twenty minutes or until they are done. Put them on a hot dish; pour off part of the gravy into another pan to make a gravy to serve with them, if you choose. Then fry apples which you have sliced about two-thirds of an inch thick, cutting them around the apple so that the core is in the centre of each piece; then cut out the core. When they are browned on one side and partly cooked, turn them carefully with a pancake turner, and finish cooking; dish around the chops or on a separate dish.

⁑JOHNNY APPLESEED'S⁑ PORK MEDALLIONS

Pork medallions and apples create a great-tasting combination!
Serve with our Centennial Scalloped Potatoes.

12-ounce pork tenderloin

1/2 teaspoon poultry seasoning

1/4 teaspoon garlic powder

1/4 teaspoon coarsely ground black pepper

1 teaspoon reduced-calorie margarine

1 green apple, unpeeled

2 teaspoons corn oil

2 teaspoons cornstarch

1 cup apple juice

Cut pork tenderloin into 1/2-inch slices. Combine poultry seasoning, garlic powder, and pepper in a small bowl; stir well. Press mixture onto both sides of pork slices. Heat margarine in a nonstick skillet. Meanwhile, core apple and cut into thin slices. Sauté apple slices in margarine, about 3 minutes. Remove from skillet and set aside. Add corn oil and pork slices to skillet and brown for 2 minutes on each side. Remove from skillet and set aside. Combine cornstarch and apple juice. Add to skillet. Heat until thickened. Add pork slices. Cover and simmer about 10 minutes. To serve, place pork slices on a serving platter. Top with apple slices; spoon sauce over all.

Preparation time: 12 minutes—Cooking time: 22 minutes

NUTRIENT INFORMATION

Servings per recipe: 4—Serving size: 1 pork chop with 1/4 apple and 1/4 cup sauce

Protein 19 g, Carbohydrate 14 g, Fat 6 g, Saturated Fat 1 g,
Cholesterol 45 mg, Sodium 72 mg, Dietary Fiber 1 g

Calories 186
From protein: 41%; From carbohydrate: 30%; From fat: 29%

Food Exchanges: 2 lean meat, 1 fruit

⁂HAWAIIAN⁂ PORK CHOPS

Pork was a very important part of the American diet in the 19th century. This simple, yet delicious, variation on pork chops will become an indispensable part of your recipe file too!

4 (4-ounce) boneless pork loin chops, cut 1 inch thick

1 cup unsweetened orange-pineapple juice

2/3 cup dry sherry

1/2 teaspoon brown sugar substitute

1/4 teaspoon dried rosemary

1/4 teaspoon garlic powder

1/4 teaspoon thyme

Bay leaf

Trim fat from pork chops. Combine juice, sherry, brown sugar substitute, rosemary, garlic powder, and thyme. Place pork chops, marinade and bay leaf in large zip-top, heavy-duty plastic bag. Close bag securely and marinate in refrigerator overnight, gently shaking bag occasionally. Remove pork chops from marinade; reserve marinade after discarding bay leaf. Place chops on rack in broiling pan so surface of meat is 4 to 5 inches from heat. Broil 11 to 13 minutes, turning and basting once with marinade.

Preparation time: 5 minutes—Marinating time: 8 hours
Cooking time: 13 minutes

NUTRIENT INFORMATION

Servings per recipe: 4—Serving size: 1 pork chop

Protein 26 g, Carbohydrate 3 g, Fat 4 g, Saturated Fat 2 g,
Cholesterol 60 mg, Sodium 80 mg, Dietary Fiber <1 g

Calories 161
From protein: 65%; From carbohydrate: 7%; From fat: 22%; From alcohol: 6%

Food Exchanges: 4 very lean meat

PORK CUTLETS

from the White House Cookbook, 1894

*C*ut them from the leg, and remove the skin; trim them and beat them, and sprinkle on salt and pepper. Prepare some beaten egg in a pan, and on a flat dish a mixture of bread crumbs, minced onion and sage. Put some lard or drippings into a frying pan over the fire, and when it boils put in the cutlets, having dipped every one first in the egg and then in the seasoning. Fry them twenty or thirty minutes, turning them often. After you have taken them out of the frying pan, skim the gravy, dredge in a little flour, give it one boil, and then pour it on the dish round the cutlets. Have apple sauce to eat with them.

Pork cutlets prepared in this manner may be stewed instead of being fried. Add to them a little water, and stew them slowly till thoroughly done, keeping them closely covered, except when you remove the lid to skim them.

LOBSTER À LA NEWBURG

from the White House Cookbook, 1894

Take one whole lobster, cut up in pieces about as large as a hickory nut. Put in the same pan with a piece of butter the size of a walnut, season with salt and pepper to taste, and thicken with heavy cream sauce; add the yolk of one egg and two oz. of sherry wine.

Cream sauce for above is made as follows: 1 oz. butter, melted in saucepan; 2 oz. flour, mixed with butter, thin down to proper consistency with boiling cream.

Rector's Oyster House, Chicago

❊LUSCIOUS❊ LOBSTER BAKE

After storms, early colonists routinely found lobsters piled up two feet high on their beaches; at that time, lobsters were so abundant and so easily gathered that they were considered suitable food only for the destitute!

4 (6-ounce) lobster tails

Cooking spray

1/4 cup fine, dry herbed breadcrumbs

1 teaspoon minced chives

1/2 teaspoon dried tarragon

1/4 teaspoon black pepper

1/4 teaspoon Tabasco® sauce

1 tablespoon plus 1 teaspoon reduced-calorie margarine, melted

4 lemon halves

Cut lengthwise through top of lobster shell; press shell open. Starting at cut end of tail, carefully loosen lobster meat from bottom of shell, keeping meat attached at end of tail. Lift meat through top shell opening and place on top of shell, being careful to keep lobster meat attached to shell at tail end. Repeat procedure with other lobster tails. Place lobster tails in a baking dish coated with cooking spray.

Combine breadcrumbs, chives, tarragon, pepper, Tabasco sauce, and margarine. Sprinkle evenly over each lobster. Bake at 400° for 17 minutes or until crumbs are golden and lobster flesh turns opaque. Garnish with half a lemon.

Preparation time: 10 minutes—Cooking time: 15 minutes

NUTRIENT INFORMATION

Servings per recipe: 4—Serving size: 1 lobster tail

Protein 33 g, Carbohydrate 7 g, Fat 3 g, Saturated Fat 1 g, Cholesterol 114 mg, Sodium 695 mg, Dietary Fiber <1 g

Calories 187
From protein: 71%; From carbohydrate: 15%; From fat: 14%

Food Exchanges: 4 very lean meat, 1 vegetable

❄ G R I L L E D   H A L I B U T ❄
W I T H   C I T R U S   S A U C E

An old Polish Proverb contends, "Fish, to taste right, must swim three times—in water, in butter and in wine in the stomach." Although this dish contains no butter or wine, it tastes right—and leaves enough extra calories for you to enjoy a glass of wine with dinner!

3/4 cup no-salt-added chicken broth

1/4 cup fresh lemon juice

1 tablespoon cornstarch

1 tablespoon parsley

1/4 teaspoon salt

1/4 teaspoon dillweed

1/4 teaspoon basil

Cooking spray

8 6-ounce halibut fillets

*C*ombine chicken broth, lemon juice, and cornstarch in a small saucepan; stir well. Bring to a boil; cook 1 minute, stirring constantly. Remove from heat. Stir in parsley, salt, dillweed, and basil; set sauce aside and keep warm.

Prepare grill by coating rack with cooking spray, taking care to keep cooking spray away from heat. Place fillets on grill rack. Cover and grill 6 minutes on each side or until the fish flakes easily when tested with a fork. Serve with warm sauce.

Preparation time: 10 minutes—Cooking time: 12 minutes

N U T R I E N T   I N F O R M A T I O N

Servings per recipe: 8—Serving size: 1 fillet with 2 tablespoons sauce

Protein 36 g, Carbohydrate 2 g, Fat 4 g, Saturated Fat 1 g, Cholesterol 54 mg, Sodium 168 mg, Dietary Fiber <1 g

Calories 188
From protein: 77%; From carbohydrate: 4%; From fat: 19%

FRIED HALIBUT

from the White House Cookbook, 1894

*F*irst fry a few thin slices of salt pork until brown in an iron
frying pan; then take it up on a hot platter and keep it warm
until the halibut is fried. After washing and drying two pounds of
sliced halibut, sprinkle it with salt and pepper, dredge it well with
flour, put it into the hot pork drippings, and fry brown on both sides;
then serve the pork with the fish.

Halibut broiled in slices is a very good way of cooking it;
broiled the same as Spanish mackerel.

❦FIESTA ORANGE❦ ROUGHY

Studies show that eating fish two or three times a week slashes your chances of heart attack; orange roughy is one of the lowest fat varieties of fish around. What a delicious way to stay healthy!

16-ounce orange roughy fillet

Cooking spray

8-ounce jar mild, thick and chunky salsa

1/4 cup chopped onion

1/4 cup chopped red pepper

4-ounce can chopped green chilies, drained

1/4 cup fresh mushrooms, sliced

1/4 cup reduced-fat, shredded cheddar cheese

*P*lace orange roughy in a baking dish coated with cooking spray. Cover with salsa and sprinkle with onion, peppers, mushrooms, and cheese. Cook, covered, in 400° oven for 15 minutes or until fish flakes easily with fork. Divide fish into 4 equal portions.

Preparation time: 10 minutes—Cooking time: 15 minutes

NUTRIENT INFORMATION

Servings per recipe: 4—Serving size: 1/4 recipe

Protein 22 g, Carbohydrate 5 g, Fat 3 g, Saturated Fat 2 g, · Cholesterol 33 mg, Sodium 644 mg, Dietary Fiber 2 g

Calories 135
From protein: 65%; Carbohydrate: 15%; From fat: 20%

Food Exchanges: 3 very lean meat, 1 vegetable

B A K E D   W H I T E   F I S H

from the White House Cookbook, 1894

Thoroughly clean the fish; cut off the head or not, as preferred; cut out the backbone from the head to within two inches of the tail, and stuff with the following: Soak stale bread in water, squeeze dry; cut in pieces a large onion, fry in butter, chop fine; add the bread, two ounces of butter, salt, pepper, and a little parsley or sage; heat through, and when taken off the fire, add the yolks of two well-beaten eggs; stuff the fish rather full, sew up with fine twine, and wrap with several coils of white tape. Rub the fish over slightly with butter; just cover the bottom of a baking pan with hot water, and place the fish in it, standing back upward, and bent in the form of an S. Serve with the following dressing: Reduce the yolks of two hard-boiled eggs to a smooth paste with two tablespoonfuls good salad oil; stir in half a teaspoon English mustard, and add pepper and vinegar to taste.

CRAB CROQUETTES

from the White House Cookbook, 1894

*P*ick the meat of boiled crabs and chop it fine. Season to taste with pepper, salt, and melted butter. Moisten it well with rich milk or cream, and then stiffen it slightly with bread or cracker crumbs. Add two or three well-beaten eggs to bind the mixture. Form the croquettes, egg and bread, crumb them and fry them delicately in boiling lard. It is better to use a wire frying basket for croquettes of all kinds.

❧COASTAL CRAB CAKES❧

Although per capita consumption of fish in the United States has increased steadily, many people feel uneasy about their skill at cooking fish at home and prefer to have it prepared in a restaurant. Give this recipe a try and you'll forget your "fear of fish!"

1 pound fresh lump crabmeat, drained

1/2 cup soft whole-wheat breadcrumbs

1/2 cup minced green onion

1/3 cup finely chopped celery

2 tablespoons fat-free mayonnaise

2 tablespoons dried parsley

1 teaspoon spicy brown mustard

1 teaspoon Tabasco® sauce

1/8 teaspoon black pepper

1/4 cup liquid egg substitute

Cooking spray

Combine crabmeat, breadcrumbs, onion, celery, mayonnaise, parsley, mustard, Tabasco sauce, pepper, and egg substitute in a bowl. Divide mixture into 6 equal portions, shaping each into a 1/2-inch thick patty. Cover and chill 1 hour.

Coat a large nonstick skillet with cooking spray; place over medium-low heat until hot. Add patties and cook 5 minutes on each side or until browned.

Preparation time: 15 minutes—Chilling time: 1 hour
Cooking time: 10 minutes

NUTRIENT INFORMATION

Servings per recipe: 6—Serving size: 1 crab cake

Protein 17 g, Carbohydrate 8 g, Fat 2 g, Saturated Fat <1 g,
Cholesterol 42 mg, Sodium 583 mg, Dietary Fiber <1 g

Calories 118
From protein: 58%; From carbohydrate: 27%; From fat: 15%

Food Exchanges: 2 very lean meat, 2 vegetable

BROILED SALMON

from the White House Cookbook, 1894

*C*ut slices from an inch to an inch and a half thick, dry them in a cloth, season with salt and pepper, dredge them in sifted flour, and broil on a gridiron rubbed with suet.

ANOTHER MODE—Cut the slices one inch thick, and season them with pepper and salt; butter a sheet of white paper, lay each slice on a separate piece, envelop them in it with their ends twisted; broil gently over a clear fire, and serve with anchovy or caper sauce. When higher seasoning is required, add a few chopped herbs and a little spice.

❊GRILLED SALMON❊ STEAKS À LA SANDY

"One cannot think well, love well, sleep well, if one has not dined well."
—Virginia Woolf

1/4 cup fat-free mayonnaise

1/4 teaspoon dillweed

1/4 teaspoon marjoram

4 4-ounce salmon steaks, 1 inch thick

Cooking spray

Combine mayonnaise, dillweed, and marjoram. Spread on both sides of salmon steaks. Coat grill rack with cooking spray, taking care to keep cooking spray away from heat. Cook salmon over medium-hot coals, with lid closed, 5 to 6 minutes on each side or until the fish flakes easily with a fork. Garnish with lemon halves and dill sprigs if desired.

Preparation time: 5 minutes—Cooking time: 12 minutes

NUTRIENT INFORMATION

Servings per recipe: 4—Serving size: 1 salmon steak

*Protein 22 g, Carbohydrate 3 g, Fat 7 g, Saturated Fat 1 g,
Cholesterol 61 mg, Sodium 239 mg, Dietary Fiber 0 g*

Calories 163
From protein: 54%; From carbohydrate: 7%; From fat: 39%

Food Exchanges: 3 very lean meat, 1 vegetable, 1 fat

⁂ SPICY SALMON ⁂ PATTIES WITH MUSTARD SAUCE

"To lengthen thy life, lessen thy meals." —Benjamin Franklin

7 3/4-ounce can no-salt-added salmon, drained and flaked

1/4 cup fine, dry herbed breadcrumbs

1/2 cup liquid egg substitute, slightly beaten

2 tablespoons lemon juice

1/4 teaspoon pepper

Cooking spray

1/2 cup finely chopped celery

1/4 cup finely chopped green onions

Mustard Sauce (recipe below)

Combine salmon, breadcrumbs, egg substitute, lemon juice, and pepper. Coat a large nonstick skillet with cooking spray; place over medium-heat until hot. Add celery and green onions; sauté until tender. Combine with salmon mixture; mix well. Coat skillet again with cooking spray; place over medium-high heat until hot. Form salmon mixture into 4 patties using 1/4 cup mixture per patty. Cook about 2 minutes on each side, until browned. Serve immediately with Mustard Sauce.

Preparation time: 15 minutes—Cooking time: 15 minutes

MUSTARD SAUCE

1 tablespoon reduced-calorie margarine

2 teaspoons whole wheat flour

1/2 cup skim milk

1/2 teaspoon dry mustard

1/2 teaspoon lemon juice

1/4 teaspoon chopped parsley

1/8 teaspoon salt

*M*elt margarine over low heat; add flour, stirring until smooth. Cook 1 minute, stirring constantly. Gradually add milk; cook over medium heat, stirring constantly until thickened and bubbly. Remove from heat; stir in mustard, lemon juice, and salt.

Preparation time: 5 minutes—Cooking time: 15 minutes

NUTRIENT INFORMATION

Servings per recipe: 4—Serving size: 1 salmon patty with 1/4 cup sauce

Protein 14 g, Carbohydrate 6 g, Fat 5 g, Saturated Fat 1 g, Cholesterol 13 mg, Sodium 152 mg, Dietary Fiber <1 g

Calories 125
From protein: 45%; From carbohydrate: 19%; From fat: 36%

Food Exchanges: 2 lean meat, 1 vegetable

SALMON CROQUETTES

from the White House Cookbook, 1894

*O*ne pound of cooked salmon (about one and a half pints when chopped), one cup of cream, two tablespoonfuls of butter, one tablespoonful of flour, three eggs, one pint of crumbs, pepper, and salt; chop the salmon fine, mix the flour and butter together, let the cream come to a boil, and stir in the flour and butter, salmon and seasoning; boil one minute; stir in one well-beaten egg, and remove from the fire; when cold make into croquettes; dip in beaten egg, roll in crumbs and fry. Canned salmon can be used.

VEAL STEW

from the White House Cookbook, 1894

Cut up two or three pounds of veal into pieces three inches long and one thick. Wash it, put it into your stewpan with two quarts of water, let it boil, skim it well, and when all the scum is removed, add pepper and salt to your taste, and a small piece of butter; pare and cut in halves twelve small Irish potatoes, put them into the stewpan; when it boils, have ready a batter made with two eggs, two spoonfuls of cream or milk, a little salt, and flour enough to make it a little thicker than for pancakes; drop this into the stew, a spoonful at a time, while it is boiling; when all is in, cover the pan closely so that no steam can escape; let it boil twenty minutes and serve in a deep dish.

⚜SICILIAN VEAL AND⚜ PEPPERS OVER RICE

A hearty, yet low-fat entrée. Serve with chilled fruit salad and hot bread for a meal that's sure to become a family favorite.

Cooking spray

1 tablespoon reduced-calorie margarine

1 pound veal, cut into 1-inch cubes

10 1/2-ounce can no-salt-added tomato purée

1 clove garlic, minced

1/2 teaspoon basil

1/2 teaspoon oregano

1/8 teaspoon black pepper

1 green pepper, sliced in thin strips

1 red pepper, sliced in thin strips

1 medium onion, thinly sliced in rings

2 1/2 cups hot, cooked brown rice

Coat a large nonstick skillet with cooking spray. Heat over medium heat until hot. Melt margarine in skillet, add veal, and brown. Stir in tomato purée, garlic, basil, oregano, and pepper. Simmer, covered for 25 minutes. Add peppers and onions. Cook, covered for 20 minutes. Serve over rice.

Preparation time: 15 minutes—Cooking time: 1 hour and 10 minutes

NUTRIENT INFORMATION

Servings per recipe: 5—Serving size: 1/5 recipe with 1/2 cup cooked rice

Protein 30 g, Carbohydrate 37 g, Fat 6 g, Saturated Fat 2 g, Cholesterol 92 mg, Sodium 91 mg, Dietary Fiber 5 g

Calories 322
From protein: 37%; From carbohydrate: 46%; From fat: 17%

Food Exchanges: 2 starch, 4 very lean meat, 1 vegetable

FRIED VEAL CUTLETS

from the White House Cookbook, 1894

*P*ut into a frying pan two or three tablespoonfuls of lard or beef drippings. When boiling hot lay in the cutlets, well seasoned with salt and pepper and dredged with flour. Brown nicely on both sides; then remove the meat, and if you have more grease than is necessary for the gravy, put it aside for further use. Reserve a tablespoonful or more and rub into it a tablespoonful of flour, with the back of the spoon, until it is a smooth, rich brown color; then add gradually a cup of cold water and season with pepper and salt. When the gravy is boiled up well, return the meat to the pan and gravy. Cover it closely and allow it to stew gently on the back of the range for fifteen minutes. This softens the meat, and with this gravy it makes a nice breakfast dish.

Another mode is to simply fry the cutlets, and afterwards turning off some of the grease they were fried in, and then adding to that left in the pan a few drops of hot water, turning the whole over the fried chops.

MEDITERRANEAN VEAL CUTLETS

Capers are the pickled buds of the caper bush commonly grown in the Mediterranean region. They provide a salty note to this veal dish.

8 (2-ounce) veal cutlets

1 teaspoon black pepper, divided

Cooking spray

1/2 teaspoon thyme

1 cup low-sodium chicken broth

1/4 teaspoon grated lemon peel

1/4 cup lemon juice

1 tablespoon plus 1 teaspoon capers

2 tablespoons water

1 teaspoon cornstarch

Place each cutlet between 2 sheets of heavy-duty plastic wrap; flatten to 1/8 inch thickness using a meat mallet or rolling pin. Sprinkle 1/2 teaspoon pepper over cutlets. Coat a large nonstick skillet with cooking spray; place over medium-high heat until hot. Add cutlets; cook 2 minutes on each side, or until done. Remove from skillet, set aside and keep warm. Add remaining 1/2 teaspoon pepper, thyme, broth, lemon peel, lemon juice, and capers to skillet; cook 2 minutes. Combine water and cornstarch; stir well and add to skillet. Bring to a boil and cook 1 minute, stirring constantly. Serve sauce over cutlets.

Preparation time: 15 minutes—Cooking time: 15 minutes

NUTRIENT INFORMATION

Servings per recipe: 4—Serving size: 2 cutlets plus 2 tablespoons sauce

Protein 32 g, Carbohydrate 2 g, Fat 5 g, Saturated Fat 2 g, Cholesterol 114 mg, Sodium 175 mg, Dietary Fiber <1 g

Calories 181
From protein: 71%; From carbohydrate: 4%; From fat: 25%

Food Exchanges: 4 very lean meat, 1 vegetable

FRIED VENISON STEAK

from the White House Cookbook, 1894

Cut a breast of venison into steaks; make a quarter of a pound of butter hot in a pan; rub the steaks over with a mixture of a little salt and pepper; dip then in wheat flour, or rolled crackers, and fry a rich brown; when both sides are done, take them up on a dish, and put a tin cover over; dredge a heaping teaspoonful of flour into the butter in the pan, stir it with a spoon until it is brown, without burning; put to it a small teacupful of boiling water, with a tablespoonful of currant jelly dissolved into it; stir it for a few minutes, then strain it over the meat and serve. A glass of wine, with a tablespoonful of white sugar dissolved in it, may be used for the gravy, instead of the jelly and water. Venison may be boiled, and served with boiled vegetables, pickled beets, etc., and sauce.

✣VENISON CUTLETS✣ WITH ORANGE SAUCE

It has been said that game made the settlement of America possible, although venison (the meat of any antlered animal) is not eaten by many in the 20th century. Modern recipes use venison in a similar manner as beef, with the best tenderizer being a tasty marinade. Another tip: reduce the gamey taste of venison by soaking it overnight in milk.

12 (4-ounce) venison cutlets

1/4 teaspoon salt

1/8 teaspoon black pepper

Cooking spray

2 tablespoons reduced-calorie margarine

1 tablespoon cognac

1/4 cup orange juice

1 tablespoon currant jelly

1/2 cup mandarin orange sections

Sprinkle cutlets with salt and pepper; spray nonstick skillet with cooking spray and heat over medium-high heat until hot. Melt margarine in skillet and sauté cutlets until brown on both sides. Remove to heated platter and keep warm. Add cognac, orange juice, and jelly to pan drippings. Mix well, bring to a boil, and cook 1 minute. Add mandarin orange sections to orange juice mixture and heat through. Spoon sauce over meat.

Preparation time: 10 minutes—Cooking time: 20 minutes

NUTRIENT INFORMATION

Servings per recipe: 6—Serving size: 2 cutlets with 1/4 cup sauce

Protein 26 g, Carbohydrate 4 g, Fat 5 g, Saturated Fat 1 g, Cholesterol 95 mg, Sodium 179 mg, Dietary Fiber <1 g

Calories 170
From protein: 61%; From carbohydrate: 9%; From fat: 26%; From alcohol: 3%

Food Exchanges: 3 very lean meat, 1 vegetable

⁂MACARONI AND⁂ CHEESE CASSEROLE

It is believed that Thomas Jefferson, our third President, brought pasta to America from France, where he had served as American ambassador!

1 1/2 cups uncooked elbow macaroni

1/4 cup chopped onion

2 tablespoons liquid Butter Buds®

2 tablespoons whole wheat flour

1/8 teaspoon black pepper

1/8 teaspoon dry mustard

1 1/2 cups skim milk

1 cup shredded, reduced-fat Swiss cheese

1 cup shredded, reduced-fat extra sharp cheddar cheese

1/4 cup chopped fresh parsley

Cooking spray

3/4 cup fine, dry breadcrumbs

1/8 teaspoon paprika

Cook macaroni according to package directions, omitting salt; drain. Rinse macaroni under cold, running water and drain again. Set macaroni aside. Sauté onion in Butter Buds in a medium saucepan until tender. Add flour, pepper, and dry mustard, stirring until smooth. Cook 1 minute, stirring constantly. Gradually add milk. Cook mixture over medium heat until thickened and bubbly. Stir in cheeses. Reduce heat and cook until cheeses melt. Remove from heat and stir in reserved macaroni and parsley. Spoon mixture into a 1 1/2-quart casserole coated with cooking spray. Sprinkle with bread crumbs and paprika. Bake at 350° for 30 minutes.

Preparation time: 10 minutes—Cooking time: 55 minutes

NUTRIENT INFORMATION

Servings per recipe: 6—Serving size: 1 cup

*Protein 19 g, Carbohydrate 27 g, Fat 7 g, Saturated Fat 4 g,
Cholesterol 28 mg, Sodium 289 mg, Dietary Fiber <1 g*

Calories 247
From protein: 31%; From carbohydrate: 44%; From fat: 26%

Food Exchanges: 2 starch, 2 lean meat

MACARONI AND CHEESE
from the White House Cookbook, 1894

Break half a pound of macaroni into pieces an inch or two long; cook it in boiling water, enough to cover it well; put in a good teaspoonful of salt; let it boil about twenty minutes. Drain it well and then put a layer in the bottom of a well-buttered pudding-dish; upon this some grated cheese and small pieces of butter, a bit of salt, then more macaroni, and so on, filling the dish; sprinkle the top layer with a thick layer of cracker crumbs. Pour over the whole a teacupful of cream or milk. Set it in the oven and bake half an hour. It should be nicely browned on top. Serve in the same dish in which it was baked with a clean napkin pinned around it.

BOILED HAM
from the White House Cookbook, 1894

First remove all the dust and mold by wiping with a coarse cloth; soak it for an hour in cold water, then wash it thoroughly. Cut with a sharp knife the hardened surface from the base and butt of the ham. Place it over the fire in cold water, and let it come to a moderate boil, keeping it steadily at this point, allowing it to cook twenty minutes for every pound of meat. A ham weighing twelve pounds will require four hours to cook properly, as underdone ham is very unwholesome. When the ham is to be served hot, remove the skin by peeling it off, place it on a platter, the fat side up, and dot the surface with spots of black pepper. Stick in also some whole cloves.

If the ham is to be served cold, allow it to remain in the pot until the water in which it was cooked becomes cold. This makes it more juicy. Serve it in the same manner as when served hot.

⊰GLAZED EASTER HAM⊱

Whenever you serve this simple and delicious recipe, you'll be reminded of your Easter dinner table. Our Santa Fe Green Beans make the perfect side dish. Remember—ham is naturally high in sodium, so save it for a special treat!

1/2 cup unsweetened orange juice

2 tablespoons golden raisins

1 cup water-packed apricots, drained

1/4 teaspoon ginger

1/8 teaspoon nutmeg

12-ounce lean ham steak, trimmed of fat

Cooking spray

Combine orange juice, raisins, apricots, ginger, and nutmeg in a small saucepan. Cook over medium heat until thickened, about 8-10 minutes. Place ham in baking pan coated with cooking spray. Pour sauce over ham. Bake at 350° for 20 minutes.

Preparation time: 5 minutes—Cooking time: 30 minutes

NUTRIENT INFORMATION

Servings per recipe: 4—Serving size: 3 ounces ham with 1/4 cup glaze

Protein 22 g, Carbohydrate 11 g, Fat 5 g, Saturated Fat 2 g, Cholesterol 47 mg, Sodium 1131 mg, Dietary Fiber 1 g

Calories 177
From protein: 50%; From carbohydrate: 25%; From fat: 25%

Food Exchanges: 1 starch, 3 very lean meat

TO KEEP MEAT FROM FLIES

from the White House Cookbook, 1894

*P*ut in sacks, with enough straw around it so the flies cannot reach through. Three-fourths of a yard of yard-wide muslin is the right size for the sack. Put a little straw in the bottom, then put in the ham and lay straw in all around it; tie it tightly and hand it in a cool, dry place. Be sure the straw is all around the meat, so the flies cannot reach through to deposit the eggs. (The sacking must be done early in the season before the fly appears.) Muslin lets the air in and is much better than paper. Thin muslin is as good as thick, and will last for years if washed when laid away when emptied.

—National Stockman

*C*arving.

Carving is one important acquisition in the routine of daily living, and all should try to attain a knowledge of ability to do it well, and withal gracefully.

When carving, use a chair slightly higher than the ordinary size, as it gives a better purchase on the meat, and appears more graceful than when standing, as is often necessary when carving a turkey, or a very large joint. More depends on skill than strength. The platter should be placed opposite, and sufficiently near to give perfect command of the article to be carved, the knife of medium size, sharp with a keen edge. Commence by cutting the slices thin, laying them carefully to one side of the platter, and then afterwards placing the desired amount on each guest's plate, to be served in turn by the servant.

A word about the care of carving knives: a fine steel knife should not come in contact with intense heat, because it destroys its temper, and therefore impairs its cutting qualities. Table carving knives should not be used in the kitchen, either around the stove, or for cutting bread, meats, vegetables, etc.; a fine whetstone should be kept for sharpening, and the knife cleaned carefully to avoid dulling its edge, all of which is quite essential to successful carving.

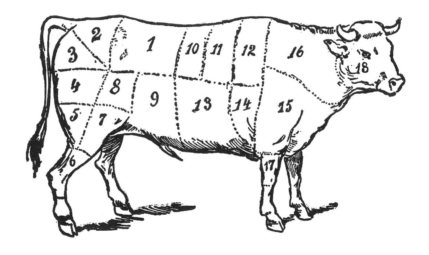

Beef Hind-Quarter.

No. 1 Used for choice roasts, the porter-house and sirloin steaks.

No. 2 Rump, used for steaks, stews, and corned beef.

No. 3 Aitch-bone, used for boiling-pieces, stews, and pot roasts.

No. 4 Buttock or round, used for steaks, pot roasts, beef à la mode; also a prime boiling-piece.

No. 5 Mouse-round, used for boiling and stewing.

No. 6 Shin or leg, used for soups, hashes, etc.

No. 7 Thick flank, cut with under fat, is a prime boiling-piece, good for stews and corned beef, pressed beef.

No. 8 Veiny piece, used for corned beef, dried beef.

No. 9 Thin flank, used for corned beef and boiling-pieces.

Fore-Quarter.

No. 10 Five ribs called the fore-rib. This is considered the primest piece for roasting; also makes the finest steaks.

No. 11 Four ribs, called the middle ribs, used for roasting.

No. 12 Chuck ribs, used for second quality of roasts and steaks.

No. 13 Brisket, used for corned beef, stews, soups, and spiced beef.

No. 14 Shoulder-piece, used for stews, soups, pot-roasts, mince-meat, and hashes.

Nos. 15, 16 Neck, clod, or sticking-piece, used for stocks, gravies, soups, mince-pie meat, hashes, bologna sausages, etc.

No. 17 Shin or shank, used mostly for soups and stewing.

No. 18 Cheek.

The following is a classification of the qualities of meat, according to the several joints of beef, when cut up.

First Class—Includes the sirloin with the kidney suet (1), the rump steak piece (2), the fore-rib (11).

Second Class—The buttock or round (4), the thick flank (7), the middle ribs (11).

Third Class—The aitch-bone (3), the mouse-round (5), the thin flank (8, 9), the chuck (12), the shoulder-piece (14), the brisket (13).

Fourth Class—The clod, neck, and sticking-piece (15, 16).

Fifth Class—Shin or shank (17).

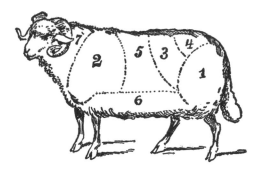

Mutton.

No. 1 Leg, used for roasts and for boiling.

No. 2 Shoulder, used for baked dishes and roasts.

No. 3 Loin, best end used for roasts, chops.

No. 4 Loin, chump-end used for roasts and chops.

No. 5 Rack, or rib chops, used for French chops, rib chops, either for frying or broiling; also used for choice stews.

No. 6 Breast, used for roast, baked dishes, stews, chops.

No. 7 Neck or scrag-end, used for cutlets, stews, and meat-pies.

Note—A saddle of mutton or double loin is two loins cut off before the carcass is split open down the back. French chops are a small rib chop, the end of the bone trimmed off and the meat and fat cut away from the thin end, leaving the round piece of meat attached to the larger end, which leaves the small rib-bone bare. Very tender and sweet.

Mutton is prime when cut from a carcass which has been fed out of doors, and allowed to run upon the hillside; they are best when about three years old. The fat will then be abundant, white and hard, the flesh juicy and firm, and of a clear red color.

For mutton roasts, choose the shoulder, the saddle, or the loin or haunch. The leg should be boiled. Almost any part will do for broth.

Lamb born in the middle of the winter, reared under shelter, and fed in a great measure upon milk, then killed in the spring, is considered a great delicacy, though lamb is good at a year old. Like all young animals, lamb ought to be thoroughly cooked, or it is most unwholesome.

Pork.

No. 1. Leg, used for smoked hams, roasts, and corned pork.

No. 2. Hind-loin, used for roasts, chops, and baked dishes.

No. 3. Fore-loin or ribs, used for roasts, baked dishes, or chops.

No. 4. Spare-rib, used for roasts, chops, stews.

No. 5. Shoulder, used for smoked shoulder, roasts, and corned pork.

No. 6. Brisket and flank, used for pickling in salt and smoked bacon.

The cheek is used for pickling in salt, also the shank or shin. The feet are usually used for souse and jelly.

For family use, the leg is the most economical, that is when fresh, and the loin the richest. The best pork is from carcasses weighing from fifty to about one hundred and twenty-five pounds. Pork is a white and close meat, and it is almost impossible to over-roast or cook it too much; when under-done it is exceedingly unwholesome.

Venison.

No. 1. Shoulder, used for roasting; it may be boned and stuffed, then afterwards baked or roasted.

No. 2. Fore-loin, used for roasts and steaks.

No. 3. Haunch or loin, used for roasts, steaks, stews. The ribs cut close may be used for soups. Food for pickling and making into smoked venison.

No. 4. Breast, used for baking dishes, stewing.

No. 5. Scrag or neck, used for soups.

The choice of venison should be judged by the fat, which, when the venison is young, should be thick, clear and close, and the meat a very dark red. The flesh of a female deer about four years old, is the sweetest and best of venison.

Buck venison, which is in season from June to the end of September, is finer than doe venison, which is in season from October to December. Neither should be dressed at any other time of year, and no meat requires so much care as venison in killing, preserving, and dressing.

*M*odes of Frying.

The usual custom among professional cooks is to entirely immerse the article to be cooked in boiling fat, but from inconvenience most households use the half-frying method of frying in a small amount of fat in a frying pan. For the first method, a shallow iron frying kettle, large at the top and small at the bottom, is best to use. The fat should half fill the kettle, or an amount sufficient to float whatever is to be fried; the heat of the fat should get to such a degree that, when a piece of bread or a teaspoonful of the batter is dropped in it, it will become brown almost instantly, but should not be so hot as to burn the fat. Some cooks say that the fat should be smoking, but my experience is, that is a mistake, as that soon ruins the fat. As soon as it begins to smoke, it should be removed a little to one side, and still be kept at the boiling point. If fritters, crullers, croquettes, etc., are dropped into fat that is too hot, it crusts over the outside before the inside has fully risen, making a heavy, hard article, and also ruining the fat, giving it a burnt flavor.

Many French cooks prefer beef fat or suet to lard for frying purposes, considering it more wholesome and digestible, does not impart as much flavor, or adhere or soak into the article cooked as pork fat.

In families of any size, where there is much cooking required, there are enough drippings and fat remnants from roasts of beef, skimmings from the soup kettle, with the addition of occasionally a pound of suet from the market, to amply supply the need. All such remnants and skimmings should be clarified about twice a week, by boiling them all together in water. When the fat is all melted, it should be strained with the water and set aside to cool. After the fat on the top has hardened, lift the cake from the water on which it lies, scrape off all the dark particles from the bottom, then melt over again the fat; while hot, strain into a small clean stone jar or bright tin pail, and then it is ready for use. Always after frying anything, the fat should stand until it settles and has cooled somewhat; then turn off carefully so as to leave it clear from the sediment that settles at the bottom.

Refined cotton-seed oil is now being adopted by most professional cooks in hotels, restaurants, and many private households for culinary purposes, and will doubtless in future supersede animal fats, especially for frying, it being quite as delicate a medium as frying with olive oil. It is now sold by leading grocers, put up in packages of two and four quarts.

The second mode of frying, using a frying pan with a small quantity of fat or grease, to be done properly, should, in the first place, have the frying pan hot over the fire, and the fat in it actually boiling before the article to be cooked is placed in it, the intense heat quickly searing up the pores of the article and forming a brown crust on the lower side, then turning over and browning the other the same way.

Still, there is another mode of frying; the process is somewhat similar to broiling, the hot frying pan or spider replacing the hot fire. To do this correctly, a thick bottomed frying pan should be used. Place it over the fire, and when it is so hot that it will hiss, oil over the bottom of the pan with a piece of suet, that is if the meat is all lean; if not, it is not necessary to grease the bottom of the pan. Lay in the meat quite flat, and brown it quickly, first on one side, then on the other; when sufficiently cooked, dish on a hot platter and season the same as broiled meats.

Management of Stoves.

If the fire in a stove has plenty of fresh coals on top not yet burned through it will need only a little shaking to start it up; but if the fire looks dying and the coals look white, don't shake it. When it has drawn till it is red again, if there is much ash and little fire, put coals on very carefully. A mere handful of fire can be coaxed back into life by adding another handful or so of new coals on the red spot, and giving plenty of draught, but don't shake a dying fire, or you lose it. This management is often necessary after a warm spell, when the stove has been kept dormant for days, though I hope you will not be so unfortunate as to have a fire to coax up on a cold winter morning. They should be arranged over night, so that all that is required is to open the draughts in order to have a cherry glow in a few minutes.

Basting the Turkey.

VEGETABLES

ASPARAGUS WITH EGGS

from the White House Cookbook, 1894

*B*oil a bunch of asparagus twenty minutes; cut off the tender tops and lay them in a deep pie plate, buttering, salting and peppering well. Beat up four eggs, the yolks and whites separately, to a stiff froth; add two tablespoonfuls of milk or cream, a tablespoonful of warm butter, pepper, and salt to taste. Pour evenly over the asparagus mixture. Bake eight minutes or until the eggs are set. Very good.

❧ALL-AMERICAN❧ ASPARAGUS

Without a heavy sauce of eggs and cream,
the natural goodness of asparagus shines through.

1/4 cup onion, diced

1/2 cup green pepper, chopped

1/2 cup red pepper, chopped

1 teaspoon salt

1/4 teaspoon black pepper

1/2 cup water

2 (10-ounce) packages frozen asparagus spears

2 teaspoons pimento, diced

1/2 teaspoon rosemary

1/2 teaspoon thyme

2 teaspoons parsley

*P*lace onion, peppers, salt, pepper, and water in a skillet. Bring to a boil. Cover and simmer 5 minutes. Add asparagus and steam for 12 to 15 more minutes. Garnish with pimento, rosemary, thyme, and parsley.

Preparation time: 5 minutes—Cooking time: 25 minutes

N U T R I E N T   I N F O R M A T I O N

Servings per recipe: 6—Serving size: 4 asparagus spears

Protein 3 g, Carbohydrate 8 g, Fat <1 g, Saturated Fat <1 g,
Cholesterol 0, Sodium 95 mg, Dietary Fiber 2 g

Calories 49
From protein: 24%; From carbohydrate: 65%; From fat: 10%

Food Exchanges: 2 vegetable

⋇IVY LEAGUE BEETS⋇

A lighter version of a classic garden vegetable dish.

2 1/2 pounds medium beets

2/3 cup unsweetened orange juice

2 tablespoons cider vinegar

1 tablespoon reduced-calorie margarine, melted

1 teaspoon brown sugar substitute

1 tablespoon cornstarch

1/4 teaspoon salt

1/4 teaspoon ground allspice

1/4 teaspoon ground ginger

1/8 teaspoon black pepper

Scrub beets with a brush, leaving root and 1 inch of stem. Place in a Dutch oven, and add water to cover; bring to a boil. Cover; reduce heat and simmer 40 minutes or until tender. Drain; peel and cut into 1/4-inch thick slices. Set aside. Combine orange juice, vinegar, and margarine in a bowl. Combine brown sugar substitute and remaining ingredients in a large saucepan; stir well. Gradually add juice mixture, stirring with a wire whisk until blended. Bring to a boil over medium heat, stirring constantly. Add beets, tossing gently to coat. Cook 4 minutes or until thoroughly heated, stirring occasionally. Serve warm.

Preparation time: 20 minutes—Cooking time: 50 minutes

NUTRIENT INFORMATION

Servings per recipe: 5—Serving size: 1 cup

*Protein 3 g, Carbohydrate 21 g, Fat 1 g, Saturated Fat <1 g,
Cholesterol 0, Sodium 247 mg, Dietary Fiber 5 g*

Calories 105
From protein: 11%; From carbohydrate: 80%; From fat: 9%

Food Exchanges: 1 starch, 1 vegetable

BEETS, BOILED

from the White House Cookbook, 1894

Select small-sized, smooth roots. They should be carefully washed, but not cut before boiling, as the juice will escape and the sweetness of the vegetable be impaired, leaving it white and hard. Put them in boiling water, and boil them until tender, which requires often from one to two hours. Do not probe them, but press them with the finger to ascertain if they are sufficiently done. When satisfied of this, take them up, and put them into a pan of cold water, and slip off the outside. Cut them into thin slices, and while hot, season with butter, salt, a little pepper, and very sharp vinegar.

LADIES' CABBAGE

from the White House Cookbook, 1894

*B*oil a firm white cabbage fifteen minutes, changing the water then for more from the boiling tea-kettle. When tender, drain and set aside until perfectly cold. Chop fine and add two beaten eggs, a tablespoonful of butter, pepper, salt, three tablespoonfuls of rich milk or cream. Stir all well together, and bake in a buttered pudding-dish until brown. Serve very hot. This dish resembles cauli-flower and is very digestible and palatable.

⚜ COLORFUL ⚜ CABBAGE SLAW

This is a cabbage recipe that ladies, as well as gentlemen, will enjoy!

3 tablespoons all-purpose flour

4 packets saccharin sugar substitute

1 teaspoon dry mustard

1 cup skim milk

1/4 cup cider vinegar

3 tablespoons lemon juice

5 cups packaged, pre-shredded cabbage

2 tablespoons golden raisins

1 medium red apple, cored and cubed

Combine flour, sugar substitute, and mustard in a small saucepan; gradually stir in milk. Cook over medium heat, stirring constantly, until mixture thickens. Remove from heat; stir in vinegar and lemon juice. Cool to room temperature. Combine cabbage, raisins, and apple in a large bowl. Pour vinegar mixture over cabbage mixture, tossing to coat well. Cover and chill thoroughly.

Preparation time: 10 minutes—Cooking time: 8 minutes
Chilling time: 3 hours

NUTRIENT INFORMATION

Servings per recipe: 6—Serving size: 1 cup

From protein: 3 g, Carbohydrate 14 g, Fat <1 g, Saturated Fat <1 g, Cholesterol 1 mg, Sodium 40 mg, Dietary Fiber 2 g

Calories 73
From protein: 16%; From carbohydrate: 77%; From fat: 7%

Food Exchanges: 1 starch

❊ S W E E T   ' N   S P I C Y ❊ C A R R O T S

*The mild, honeylike flavor of carrots is enhanced
by the addition of Dijon mustard.*

1 pound baby carrots, scraped

2 tablespoons reduced-calorie margarine, melted

1 tablespoon Dijon mustard

1 tablespoon honey

1/4 teaspoon ground allspice

1/4 teaspoon ground nutmeg

*P*lace carrots in a medium saucepan and cover with water. Bring to a
boil and cook carrots until crisp-tender, about 12 minutes. Drain
and keep warm. Combine margarine, mustard, honey, allspice, and
nutmeg; stir well. Pour over carrots and toss gently to coat.

Preparation time: 5 minutes—Cooking time: 12 minutes

N U T R I E N T   I N F O R M A T I O N

Servings per recipe: 4—Serving size: 1 cup

*Protein 1 g, Carbohydrate 16 g, Fat 2 g, Saturated Fat <1 g,
Cholesterol 0, Sodium 121 mg, Dietary Fiber 3 g*

Calories 86
From protein: 5%; From carbohydrate: 74%; From fat: 21%

Food Exchanges: 1 starch

STEWED CARROTS

from the White House Cookbook, 1894

Wash and scrape the carrots and divide them into strips; put them into a stewpan with water enough to cover them; add a spoonful of salt and let them boil slowly until tender; then drain and replace them in the pan, with two tablespoonfuls of butter rolled in flour, shake over a little pepper and salt; then add enough cream or milk to moisten the whole; let it come to a boil and serve hot.

CORN CASSEROLE

*A favorite traditional side dish—without the high
cholesterol content of the 1890s' version.*

1 tablespoon reduced-calorie margarine

1/2 cup diced green onions

1/4 cup diced green pepper

1/4 cup diced red pepper

2 1/4 cups 1% low-fat milk

1 tablespoon plus 1 teaspoon sugar

3/4 teaspoon salt

1/4 teaspoon cayenne pepper

1/3 cup plus 1 tablespoon all-purpose flour

1/2 cup liquid egg substitute

3 egg whites, lightly beaten

3 1/2 cups frozen whole kernel corn, thawed

Cooking spray

2 tablespoons fine, dry breadcrumbs

Melt margarine in a saucepan over medium heat. Add green onions
and peppers; sauté for 1 minute. Add milk, sugar, salt, and cayenne
pepper. Cook 3 minutes or until hot. Do not boil. Remove from heat and set
aside. Combine flour, egg substitute, and egg whites in a bowl. Beat at
medium speed with an electric mixer until well blended. Gradually stir in
1/2 cup of the hot milk mixture; continue to gradually add the remaining hot
milk mixture, stirring constantly. Stir in the corn and pour into a shallow
2-quart casserole which has been coated with cooking spray. Bake at 350° for
20 minutes; remove from oven, stir and bake for an additional 10 minutes.
Remove from oven, top with breadcrumbs, and bake for an additional
5 minutes or until a knife inserted near the center comes out clean.

Preparation time: 15 minutes—Cooking time: 35 minutes

NUTRIENT INFORMATION

Servings per recipe: 6—Serving size: 1 cup

*Protein 11 g, Carbohydrate 36 g, Fat 3 g, Saturated Fat 1 g,
Cholesterol 4 mg, Sodium 340 mg, Dietary Fiber 3 g*

Calories 215
From protein: 20%; From carbohydrate: 67%; From fat: 13%

Food Exchanges: 2 starch, 1 vegetable, 1 fat

CORN PUDDING

from the White House Cookbook, 1894

This is a Virginia dish. Scrape the substance out of twelve ears of tender, green, uncooked corn (it is better scraped than grated, as you do not get those husky particles which you cannot avoid with a grater); add yolks and whites, beaten separately, of four eggs, a teaspoonful of sugar, the same of flour mixed in a tablespoonful of butter, a small quantity of salt and pepper, and one pint of milk. Bake about half or three-quarters of an hour.

STEWED CORN
from the White House Cookbook, 1894

Take a dozen ears of green sweet corn, very tender and juicy; cut off the kernels, cutting with a large sharp knife from the top of the cob down; then scrape the cob. Put the corn in a saucepan over the fire with just enough water to make it cook without burning; boil about twenty minutes, then add a teacupful of milk or cream, a tablespoonful of cold butter, and season with pepper and salt. Boil ten minutes longer and dish up hot in a vegetable dish. The corn would be much sweeter if the scraped cobs were boiled first in the water that the corn is cooked in.

Many like corn cooked in this manner, putting half corn and half tomatoes; either way is very good.

⊰SOUTHWESTERN⊱ CORN ON THE COB

This quick and spicy side dish is especially tasty with grilled meats.

1 tablespoon plus 1 teaspoon hot water

2 teaspoons reduced-calorie margarine, melted

1/2 teaspoon chili powder

1/2 teaspoon ground cumin

1/2 teaspoon paprika

1/4 teaspoon garlic salt

1/8 teaspoon cayenne pepper

6 frozen ears corn on the cob

Combine water, margarine, chili powder, cumin, paprika, garlic salt, and cayenne pepper in a small bowl; stir well. Cook corn according to package directions. Brush margarine mixture over corn before serving.

Preparation time: 5 minutes—Cooking time: 12 minutes

NUTRIENT INFORMATION

Servings per recipe: 6—Serving size: 1 ear of corn

Protein 4 g, Carbohydrate 29 g, Fat 2 g, Saturated Fat < 1 g, Cholesterol 0, Sodium 110 mg, Dietary Fiber 3 g

Calories 150
From protein: 11%; From carbohydrate: 77%; From fat: 12%

Food Exchanges: 2 starch

❈ITALIAN EGGPLANT❈ BAKE

Eggplant parmesan with less of the fat, but all of the taste.

1/2 cup dry white wine

2 teaspoons dried basil

2 teaspoons dried oregano

1/4 teaspoon salt

32 ounces no-salt-added tomato sauce

28 ounces no-salt-added diced tomatoes, undrained

6 ounces no-salt-added tomato paste

1/2 cup minced onion

2 garlic cloves, minced

2 (1-pound) eggplants, cut into 1/4-inch slices

1/4 cup water

3 egg whites, lightly beaten

1 1/4 cups Italian-seasoned breadcrumbs

1/4 cup grated Parmesan cheese

Cooking spray

1 1/2 cups shredded part-skim mozzarella cheese

1 1/2 cups shredded fat-free mozzarella cheese

Combine wine, basil, oregano, salt, tomato sauce, whole tomatoes, tomato paste, onions, and garlic in a large saucepan; bring to a boil. Reduce heat and simmer, uncovered, 20 minutes. Place eggplant in a large bowl. Add enough very cold water to cover and let stand 30 minutes. Drain well; blot dry with paper towels. Combine 1/4 cup water and egg whites in a shallow bowl. In a separate bowl, combine breadcrumbs and Parmesan cheese; stir well. Dip eggplant in egg-white mixture and dredge in breadcrumb mixture. Place half of eggplant slices on a baking sheet coated with cooking spray and broil 5 minutes on each side or until browned. Repeat procedure with remaining eggplant. Set eggplant aside. Spread half of tomato mixture in bottom of a 9" x 13" baking dish coated with cooking spray. Arrange half of eggplant over

FRIED EGG-PLANT

from the White House Cookbook, 1894

Take fresh, purple egg-plants of a middling size; cut them in slices a quarter of an inch thick, and soak them for half an hour in cold water, with a teaspoonful of salt in it. Have ready some cracker or bread crumbs and one beaten egg; drain off the water from the slices, lay them on a napkin, dip them in the crumbs and then in the egg, put another coat of crumbs on them and fry them in butter to a light brown. The frying pan must be hot before the slices are put in; they will fry in ten minutes.

You may pare them before you put them into the frying pan, or you may pull off the skins when you take them up. You must not remove them from the water until you are ready to cook them, as the air will turn them black.

sauce; top with half of mozzarella cheeses. Repeat layers with remaining sauce, eggplant, and cheese. Bake at 350° for 30 minutes or until bubbly. Let stand 5 minutes before serving. Garnish with minced parsley or oregano, if desired.

Preparation time: 20 minutes—Cooking time: 1 hour and 10 minutes
Standing time: 35 minutes

NUTRIENT INFORMATION

Servings per recipe: 8—Serving size: 1/8 pan

Protein 22 g, Carbohydrate 36 g, Fat 6 g, Saturated Fat 3 g,
Cholesterol 14 mg, Sodium 675 mg, Dietary Fiber 3 g

Calories 291
From protein: 30%; From carbohydrate: 49%; From fat: 19%; From alcohol: 2%

Food Exchanges: 2 starch, 2 very lean meat, 1 vegetable

GREENS

from the White House Cookbook, 1894

About a peck of greens are enough for a mess for a family of six, such as dandelions, cowslips, burdock, chicory, and other greens. All greens should be carefully examined, the tough ones thrown out, then be thoroughly washed through several waters until they are entirely free from sand. The addition of a handful of salt to each pan of water used in washing the greens will free them from insects and worms, especially if after the last watering they are allowed to stand in salted water for a half hour or longer. When ready to boil the greens, put them into a large pot half full of boiling water, with a handful of salt, and boil them steadily until the stalks are tender; this will be in from five to twenty minutes, according to the maturity of the greens; but remember that long-continued boiling wastes the tender substances of the leaves, and so diminishes both the bulk and the nourishment of the dish; for this reason it is best to cut away any tough stalks before beginning to cook the greens. As soon as they are tender, drain them in a colander, chop them a little and return them to the fire long enough to season them with salt, pepper and butter; vinegar may be added if it is liked; the greens should be served as soon as they are hot. All kinds of greens can be cooked in this manner.

MUSTARD GREENS WITH ROASTED CHICKEN

Mustard greens are an excellent source of calcium.
In this recipe, they add good taste as well as good nutrition.

1 1/2 pounds fresh mustard greens

1 teaspoon olive oil

1 clove garlic, minced

1/2 cup green pepper, thinly sliced

1/2 cup red pepper, thinly sliced

1/2 pound fresh mushrooms, sliced

2 ounces julienne-cut roasted chicken breast

*R*emove stems from mustard greens and rinse thoroughly. Coarsely chop and set aside. Heat olive oil in a large skillet over medium heat until hot; add greens and garlic. Cover and cook 10 minutes, stirring occasionally. Add peppers, mushrooms, and chicken breast, tossing gently. Cover and cook an additional 5 minutes. Serve with a slotted spoon.

Preparation time: 10 minutes—Cooking time: 20 minutes

NUTRIENT INFORMATION

Servings per recipe: 4—Serving size: 1 cup

Protein 9 g, Carbohydrate 11 g, Fat 2 g, Saturated Fat <1 g,
Cholesterol 11 mg, Sodium 200 mg, Dietary Fiber 5 g

Calories 98
From protein: 37%; From carbohydrate: 45%; From fat: 18%

Food Exchanges: 1 starch, 1 very lean meat

⁂TABASCO⁂ MUSHROOMS

The mild flavor of mushrooms complemented many dishes 100 years ago; of course, cooks went to great lengths to be absolutely sure that the wild mushrooms brought to their kitchens were not poisonous!

3 tablespoons water

2 teaspoons Tabasco® sauce

2 teaspoons prepared spicy brown mustard

1/4 teaspoon paprika

1 large onion, thinly sliced and separated into rings

Cooking spray

1 1/2 cups presliced fresh mushrooms

Combine water, Tabasco sauce, mustard, and paprika in a large bowl; stir well. Add onion rings, tossing gently to coat. Coat a large nonstick skillet with cooking spray. Place over medium heat until hot. Add onion mixture. Cook 5 minutes, stirring constantly. Add mushrooms; cook 5 minutes or until mushrooms are tender, stirring constantly.

Preparation time: 5 minutes—Cooking time: 10 minutes

NUTRIENT INFORMATION

Servings per recipe: 4—Serving size: 1/2 cup

Protein 1 g, Carbohydrate 5 g, Fat 1 g, Saturated Fat <1 g, Cholesterol 0, Sodium 46 mg, Dietary Fiber 1 g

Calories 29
From protein: 14%; From carbohydrate: 69%; From fat: 17%

Food Exchanges: 1 vegetable

STEWED MUSHROOMS

from the White House Cookbook, 1894

Time, twenty-one minutes. Button mushrooms, salt to taste, a little butter rolled in flour, two tablespoonfuls of cream or the yolk of one egg. Choose buttons of uniform size. Wipe them clean and white with a wet flannel; put them in a stewpan with a little water and let them stew very gently for a quarter of an hour. Add salt to taste, work in a little flour and butter, to make the liquor about as thick as cream, and let it boil for five minutes. When you are ready to dish it up, stir in two tablespoonfuls of cream of the yolk of an egg; stir it over the fire for a minute, but do not let it boil, and serve.

Stewed button mushrooms are very nice, either in fish stews or ragouts, or served apart to eat with fish. Another way of doing them is to stew them in milk and water (after they are rubbed white); add to them a little veal gravy, mace, and salt; and thicken the gravy with cream of the yolks of egg.

Mushrooms can be cooked in the same manner as the recipes for oysters, either stewed, fried, broiled, or as a soup. They are also used to flavor sauces, catsups, meat gravies, game, and soups.

OKRA
from the White House Cookbook, 1894

This grows in the shape of pods, and is of a gelatinous character, much used for soup, and is also pickled; it may be boiled as follows: Put the young and tender pods of long white okra in salted boiling water in granite, porcelain, or a tin-lined saucepan—as contact with iron will discolor it; boil fifteen minutes; remove the stems, and serve with butter, pepper, salt, and vinegar if preferred.

⸙ S O U T H E R N   O K R A ⸙ S L I C E S

*Southern creole cuisine features many dishes which contain okra,
such as gumbos and soups. Enjoy okra a new way!*

1/2 pound okra

1/2 cup liquid egg substitute

3/4 cup all-purpose flour

1 1/2 teaspoons Cajun spice mix

Cooking spray

Wash okra; remove ends. Cut okra into 1/2-inch slices. Place egg substitute in a small bowl. In another small bowl combine flour and spice mix. Dip each okra slice into the egg substitute mixture, then coat with flour mixture. Spray a medium nonstick skillet with cooking spray and heat until hot. Fry okra in a single layer over medium-high heat 4 to 5 minutes, turning once, until golden brown

Preparation time: 15 minutes—Cooking time: 5 minutes

N U T R I E N T   I N F O R M A T I O N

Servings per recipe: 4—Serving size: 1 cup

*Protein 7 g, Carbohydrate 22 g, Fat 2 g, Saturated Fat <1 g,
Cholesterol <1 mg, Sodium 61 mg, Dietary Fiber 2 g*

Calories 134
From protein: 21%; From carbohydrate: 66%; From fat: 13%

Food Exchanges: 1 starch, 1 vegetable

⁂HEAVEN-SENT PEAS⁂

The flavor of peas is said to be so delightful that legend has it they were first grown in the Garden of Eden. Enjoy this fat-free taste of heaven!

2 cups water

2 cups frozen green peas

2 tablespoons minced fresh onion

2 tablespoons diced celery

1/4 teaspoon rosemary

1/4 teaspoon tarragon

1/4 teaspoon black pepper

*B*ring water to a boil in a small saucepan and add peas, onion, and celery. Cook about 5 minutes or until celery and peas are crisp-tender. Drain. Add rosemary, tarragon, and pepper; toss gently.

Preparation time: 5 minutes—Cooking time: 5 minutes

NUTRIENT INFORMATION

Servings per recipe: 4—Serving size: 1/2 cup

Protein 4 g, Carbohydrate 12 g, Fat 0, Saturated Fat 0, Cholesterol 0, Sodium 77 mg, Dietary Fiber 3 g

Calories 64
From protein: 25%; From carbohydrate: 75%; From fat: 0

Food Exchanges: 2 vegetable

GREEN PEAS
from the White House Cookbook, 1894

Shell the peas and wash in cold water. Put in boiling water
just enough to cover them well and keep them from
burning; boil from twenty minutes to half an hour, when the liquor
should be nearly boiled out; season with pepper and salt and a
good allowance of butter; serve very hot.

This is a very much better way than cooking in a larger quantity
of water and draining off the liquor, as that diminishes the sweetness,
and much of the fine flavor of the peas is lost. The salt should
never be put in the peas before they are tender, unless very young,
as it tends to harden them.

PORK AND BEANS
(BAKED)

from the White House Cookbook, 1894

*T*ake two quarts of white beans, pick them over the night before, and put to soak in cold water; in the morning put them in fresh water and let them scald, then turn off the water and put on more, hot; put to cook with them a piece of salt pork, gashed, as much as would make five or six slices; boil slowly till soft (not mashed), then add a tablespoonful of molasses, half a teaspoonful of soda, stir in well, put in a deep pan, and bake one hour and a half. If you do not like to use pork, salt the beans when boiling, and add a lump of butter when preparing them for the oven.

⁂VERMONT⁂ BAKED BEANS

Quick and easy pork and beans with a maple syrup twist!

3 cups canned navy beans, undrained

1 tablespoon no-salt-added tomato paste

1 large onion, diced

1 tablespoon cider vinegar

2 tablespoons maple syrup

1 teaspoon dry mustard

1/8 teaspoon cayenne pepper

Combine all ingredients in a baking dish coated with cooking spray and stir well. Cover and bake at 350° for 30 minutes. Remove cover and bake for an additional 30 minutes.

Preparation time: 10 minutes— Cooking time: 1 hour

NUTRIENT INFORMATION

Servings per recipe: 8—Serving size: 3/4 cup

Protein 8 g, Carbohydrate 26 g, Fat 1 g, Saturated Fat <1 g, Cholesterol 0, Sodium 442 mg, Dietary Fiber 1 g

Calories 145
From protein: 22%; From carbohydrate: 72%; From fat: 6%

Food Exchanges: 1 starch, 2 vegetable

❊ SAVORY NEW ❊ POTATOES

"What I say is that, if a man really likes potatoes, he must be a pretty decent sort of fellow." —A.A. Milne

1 pound small new potatoes

1/2 cup plain nonfat sour cream

1 tablespoon prepared horseradish

1/8 teaspoon dried dillweed

1/4 teaspoon paprika

2 tablespoons chopped fresh chives

*R*inse potatoes and pat dry. Pierce potatoes several times with a fork and place in a ring on a paper towel in microwave oven. Microwave at HIGH 3 1/2 minutes, turn potatoes over and microwave an additional 3 1/2 minutes. Let stand 5 minutes. Cut potatoes in half lengthwise; set aside. Combine sour cream, horseradish, dillweed, and paprika in a small bowl, stirring well. Spoon 1 teaspoon sour cream mixture over each potato half. Garnish with chives.

Preparation time: 5 minutes—Cooking time: 7 minutes
Standing time: 5 minutes

NUTRIENT INFORMATION

Servings per recipe: 4—Serving size: 4 potato halves

Protein 4 g, Carbohydrate 23 g, Fat <1 g, Saturated Fat <1 g,
Cholesterol 0, Sodium 68 mg, Dietary Fiber 2 g

Calories 113
From protein: 14%; From carbohydrate: 81%; From fat: 4%

Food Exchanges: 1 starch, 1 vegetable

LYONNAISE POTATOES

from the White House Cookbook, 1894

Take eight or ten good-sized cold boiled potatoes, slice them end-wise, then crosswise, making them like dice in small squares. When you are ready to cook them, heat some butter or good drippings in a frying pan; fry in it one small onion (chopped fine) until it begins to change color and look yellow. Now put in your potatoes, sprinkle well with salt and pepper, stir well and cook about five minutes, taking care that you do not break them. They must not brown. Just before taking up stir in a tablespoonful of minced parsley. Drain dry by shaking in a heated colander. Serve very hot.

—*Delmonico*

MASHED POTATOES

from the White House Cookbook, 1894

*T*ake the quantity needed, pare off the skins and lay them in cold water half an hour; then put them into a saucepan with a little salt; cover with water and boil them until done. Drain off the water and mash them fine with a potato masher. Have ready a piece of butter the size of an egg, melted in half a cup of boiling hot milk and a good pinch of salt; mix it well with the mashed potatoes until they are a smooth paste, taking care that they are not too wet. Put them into a vegetable dish, heaping them up and smooth over the top, put a small piece of butter on the top in the centre, and have dots of pepper here and there on the surface as large as a half dime.

Some prefer using a heavy fork or wire beater, instead of a potato masher, beating the potatoes quite light and heaping them up in the dish without smoothing over the top.

⚛MODERN MASHED⚛ POTATOES

A savory mixture of herbs and spices gives this version of mashed potatoes a thoroughly modern taste.

1 1/3 pounds peeled baking potatoes, cut into 1 inch cubes

1/2 cup light cream cheese

1/4 cup skim milk

2 tablespoons dried chives

1/4 teaspoon salt

1/4 teaspoon black pepper

*I*n a medium covered saucepan, cook potatoes in 2 inches of boiling water for about 12 minutes, until tender. Drain thoroughly. Mash potatoes with a potato masher or an electric mixer. Mix in cream cheese until melted. Gently mix in skim milk, chives, salt, and pepper, being careful not to overbeat the potatoes. Stir gently over low heat until just heated through.

Preparation time: 15 minutes—Cooking time: 15 minutes

NUTRIENT INFORMATION

Servings per recipe: 4—Serving size: 1 cup

Protein 7 g, Carbohydrate 31 g, Fat 5 g, Saturated Fat 3 g, Cholesterol 11 mg, Sodium 311 mg, Dietary Fiber 2 g

Calories 197
From protein: 14%; From carbohydrate: 63%; From fat: 23%

Food Exchanges: 2 starch, 1 fat

❧ SPICY BAKED CHIPS ❧

"If you have formed the habit of checking on every new diet that comes along, you will find, mercifully, they all blur together, leaving you with only one definite piece of information: french-fried potatoes are out."—Jean Kerr

1 1/2 pounds unpeeled baking potatoes

1/2 teaspoon paprika

1/2 teaspoon onion powder

1/4 teaspoon garlic salt

1/8 teaspoon cayenne pepper

Cooking spray

*R*inse potatoes and pat dry. Cut into 1/4 inch thick slices and pat dry with paper towels. Combine paprika, onion powder, garlic salt, and pepper in a large bowl. Add potato slices and toss to coat. Arrange potatoes in a single layer on a baking sheet coated with cooking spray. Bake at 425° for 20 minutes.

Preparation time: 15 minutes—Cooking time: 20 minutes

NUTRIENT INFORMATION

Servings per recipe: 5—Serving size: 1/2 cup

Protein 3 g, Carbohydrate 25 g, Fat <1 g, Saturated Fat <1 g, Cholesterol 0, Sodium 111 mg, Dietary Fiber 2 g

Calories 117
From protein: 10%; From carbohydrate: 85%; From fat: 4%

Food Exchanges: 1 starch, 1 vegetable

SARATOGA CHIPS

from the White House Cookbook, 1894

*P*eel good-sized potatoes, and slice them as evenly as possible. Drop them into ice-water; have a kettle of very hot lard, as for cakes; put a few at a time into a towel and shake, to dry the moisture out of them, and then drop them into the boiling lard. Stir them occasionally, and when of a light brown take them out with a skimmer and they will be crisp and not greasy. Sprinkle salt over them while hot.

⁂CENTENNIAL⁂ SCALLOPED POTATOES

*These scalloped potatoes have been "lightened up"
by using skim milk and reduced-fat cheese.*

Cooking spray

1 clove garlic, minced

1/4 cup onion, diced

2 1/2 teaspoons all-purpose flour

6 ounces evaporated skim milk

3/4 cup skim milk

1/4 teaspoon salt

1/4 teaspoon cayenne pepper

2 1/2 pounds red potatoes, peeled and thinly sliced

1/2 cup shredded reduced-fat swiss cheese

1/3 cup Parmesan cheese

1/2 cup fine, dry breadcrumbs

2 tablespoons parsley

In a nonstick saucepan coated with cooking spray, sauté garlic and onion until tender. Add flour and mix well. Add evaporated milk, skim milk, salt, and pepper. Cook sauce until slightly thickened, whisking constantly, about 2 minutes. Spray a 2-quart baking dish with cooking spray. Alternate layers of potato, cheeses, and sauce. Top with breadcrumbs. Bake at 350° for 45 minutes or until bubbly and golden brown. Sprinkle with parsley. Let stand 20 minutes before serving.

*Preparation time: 15 minutes—Cooking time: 45 minutes
Standing time: 20 minutes*

NUTRIENT INFORMATION

Servings per recipe: 8—Serving size: 1 cup

*Protein 10 g, Carbohydrate 35 g, Fat 3 g, Saturated Fat 1 g,
Cholesterol 8 mg, Sodium 280 mg, Dietary Fiber 2 g*

Calories 207
From protein: 19%; From carbohydrate: 68%; From fat: 13%

Food Exchanges: 2 starch, 1 vegetable

SCALLOPED POTATOES (KENTUCKY-STYLE)

from the White House Cookbook, 1894

Peel and slice raw potatoes thin, the same as for frying. Butter an earthen dish, put in a layer of potatoes, and season with salt, pepper, butter, and a bit of onion chopped fine, if liked; sprinkle a little flour. Now put another layer of potatoes and the seasoning. Continue in this way till the dish is filled. Just before putting into the oven, pour a quart of hot milk over. Bake three-quarters of an hour.

Cold boiled potatoes may be cooked the same. It requires less time to bake them; they are delicious either way. If the onion is disliked, it can be omitted.

SPINACH

from the White House Cookbook, 1894

*I*t should be cooked so as to retain its bright green color and not be sent to table, as it so often is, of a dull brown or olive color; to retain its fresh appearance, do not cover the vessel while it is cooking.

Spinach requires close examination and picking, as insects are frequently found among it and it is often gritty. Wash it through three or four waters. Then drain it and put it in boiling water. Fifteen to twenty minutes is generally sufficient time to boil spinach. Be careful to remove the scum. When it is quite tender, take it up, and drain and squeeze it well. Chop it fine, and put it into a saucepan with a piece of butter and a little pepper and salt. Set it on the fire and let it stew five minutes, stirring it all the time, until quite dry. Turn it into a vegetable dish, shape it into a mound, slice some hard-boiled eggs and lay around the top.

❋QUICK SPINACH❋ AND MUSHROOMS

Prepackaged spinach and mushrooms are timesavers.
Quick-cooking the spinach keeps nutrients—and flavor—intact.

Cooking spray

1 cup presliced fresh mushrooms

1 small purple onion, thinly sliced and separated into rings

1/4 teaspoon ground ginger

1 teaspoon sesame seeds

1 clove garlic, minced

1/4 cup water

1 teaspoon cornstarch

1/2 teaspoon sugar

1/8 teaspoon cayenne pepper

1 tablespoon low-sodium soy sauce

1/2 teaspoon dark sesame oil

10-ounce bag prepackaged fresh spinach

Coat a large Dutch oven with cooking spray; place over medium-high heat until hot. Add mushrooms, onion, ginger, sesame seeds, and garlic; sauté 5 minutes. Combine water with cornstarch, sugar, pepper, soy sauce, and sesame oil; stir well. Add thoroughly washed and drained spinach. Cook about 2 minutes while stirring constantly until spinach begins to wilt.

Preparation time: 5 minutes—Cooking time: 8 minutes

N U T R I E N T   I N F O R M A T I O N

Servings per recipe: 6—Serving size: 1/2 cup

Protein 2 g, Carbohydrate 6 g, Fat 1 g, Saturated Fat <1 g,
Cholesterol 0, Sodium 127 mg, Dietary Fiber 2 g

Calories 41
From protein: 20%; From carbohydrate: 59%; From fat: 22%

Food Exchanges: 1 vegetable

⁂SQUASH POTPOURRI⁂

A perfect use for the bounty from your summer garden!

Cooking spray
1 tablespoon reduced-calorie margarine
1 clove garlic, minced
1 red pepper, seeded and cut into strips
1 green pepper, seeded and cut into strips
2 small yellow squash, cut into 1/4 inch slices
1 small zucchini, sliced
1 cup diced onion
1/4 teaspoon oregano
1/4 teaspoon salt
1/8 teaspoon black pepper

Coat a large nonstick skillet with cooking spray; add margarine and place over medium heat until margarine melts. Add garlic; cook 1 minute, stirring constantly. Add peppers, yellow squash, and zucchini. Cover and cook 4 minutes. Stir in onions, oregano, salt, and pepper. Cover and cook 1 minute or until vegetables are crisp-tender.

Preparation time: 15 minutes—Cooking time: 8 minutes

NUTRIENT INFORMATION

Servings per recipe: 4—Serving size: 1 cup

Protein 2 g, Carbohydrate 11 g, Fat 2 g, Saturated Fat <1 g, Cholesterol 0, Sodium 171 mg, Dietary Fiber 2 g

Calories 70
From protein: 11%; From carbohydrate: 63%; From fat: 26%

Food Exchanges: 1 starch

SQUASHES, OR CYMBLINGS

from the White House Cookbook, 1894

The green or summer squash is best when the outside is beginning to turn yellow, as it is then less watery and insipid than when younger. Wash them, cut them into pieces and take out the seeds. Boil them about three-quarters of an hour, or till quite tender. When done, drain and squeeze them well till you have pressed out all the water; mash them with a little butter, pepper and salt. Then put the squash thus prepared into a stewpan, set it on hot coals and stir it very frequently till it becomes dry. Take care not to let it burn.

Summer squash is very nice steamed, then prepared the same as boiled.

BAKED WINTER SQUASH

from the White House Cookbook, 1894

Cut open the squash, take out the seeds, and without paring cut it up into large pieces; put the pieces on tins or in a dripping-pan, place in a moderately hot oven and bake about an hour. When done, peel and mash like mashed potatoes, or serve the pieces hot on a dish, to be eaten warm with butter like sweet potatoes. It retains its sweetness much better baked this way than when boiled.

❧ HONEY-BAKED ❧ SQUASH

This makes an excellent side dish for a traditional turkey dinner.

2 medium acorn squash (about 1 pound each)

1/4 cup honey

1 tablespoon lemon juice

1/4 teaspoon allspice

Cut each squash in half lengthwise; discard seeds and membrane. Combine honey, lemon juice, and allspice. Spoon into squash shells. Place squash in an 11" x 7" x 2" baking dish. Cover dish and bake at 350° for 1 hour and 10 minutes, basting occasionally with the honey mixture. Uncover dish and bake an additional 5 minutes or until squash is tender.

Preparation time: 5 minutes   Cooking time: 1 hour and 15 minutes

NUTRIENT INFORMATION

Servings per recipe: 4—Serving size: 1 squash half

Protein 2 g, Carbohydrate 42 g, Fat <1 g, Saturated Fat <1 g, Cholesterol 0, Sodium 9 mg, Dietary Fiber 4 g

Calories 178
From protein: 4%; From carbohydrate: 94%; From fat: 1%

Food Exchanges: 1 starch, 2 other carbohydrate

❋SANTA FE GREEN❋ BEANS

*Green beans with a fiery twist. Use them as
a side dish to spice up a favorite entrée.*

2 (9-ounce) packages frozen cut green beans
1/4 cup chili sauce
1 tablespoon prepared horseradish
1/8 teaspoon black pepper
1 tablespoon reduced-calorie margarine
4 green onions, chopped

Cook green beans according to package directions, eliminating salt. Mix chili sauce, horseradish, and pepper together in a small bowl. Stir margarine, onions, and chili sauce mixture into beans. Cook 2 to 3 minutes, stirring occasionally, until just heated through.

Preparation time: 5 minutes—Cooking time: 11 minutes

NUTRIENT INFORMATION:

Servings per recipe: 6—Serving size: 1/2 cup

*Protein 2 g, Carbohydrate 10 g, Fat 1 g, Saturated Fat <1 g,
Cholesterol 0, Sodium 186 mg, Dietary Fiber 2 g*

*Calories 57
From protein: 14%; From carbohydrate: 70%; From fat: 16%*

Food Exchanges: 2 vegetable

S T R I N G   B E A N S
from the White House Cookbook, 1894

*B*reak off the end that grew to the vine, drawing off at the same time the string upon the edge; repeat the same process from the other end; cut them with a sharp knife into pieces half an inch long, and boil them in just enough water to cover them. They usually require one hour's boiling; but this depends upon their age and freshness. After they have boiled until tender and the water boiled nearly out, add pepper and salt, a tablespoonful of butter and a half a cup of cream; if you have not the cream add more butter.

Many prefer to drain them before adding the seasoning; in that case they lose the real goodness of the vegetable.

SUCCOTASH

from the White House Cookbook, 1894

Take a pint of fresh shelled Lima beans, or any large fresh beans, and put them in a pot with cold water, rather more than will cover them. Scrape the kernels from twelve ears of young sweet corn; put the cobs in with the beans, boiling from half to three-quarters of an hour. Now take out the cobs and put in the scraped corn; boil again fifteen minutes, then season with salt and pepper to taste, a piece of butter the size of an egg and half a cup of cream. Serve hot.

❧SUCCOTASH❧ IN A FLASH

Succotash was originally a North American Indian dish, going back to a simple era of cooking when everything was boiled together in one pot.

2 tablespoons reduced-calorie margarine

1/4 cup minced onion

15-ounce can no-salt-added lima beans, drained

15-ounce can no-salt-added sweet corn, drained

2 tablespoons chopped fresh parsley

1/8 teaspoon salt

1/8 teaspoon black pepper

2 tablespoons pimento

Melt margarine in a saucepan over medium-high heat. Add onion and sauté 2 minutes. Remove from heat. Stir in lima beans, corn, parsley, salt, pepper, and pimento. Return to burner and cook an additional 5 minutes or until just heated through.

Preparation time: 5 minutes—Cooking time: 7 minutes

NUTRIENT INFORMATION

Servings per recipe: 8—Serving size: 1/2 cup

Protein 4 g, Carbohydrate 20 g, Fat 2 g, Saturated Fat <1 g, Cholesterol 0, Sodium 76 mg, Dietary Fiber 4 g

Calories 114
From protein: 14%; From carbohydrate: 70%; From fat: 16%

Food Exchanges: 1 starch, 1 vegetable

❧SWEET POTATO❦ SOUFFLE

This recipe takes advantage of the time-saving food processor, a modern convenience not available to cooks a century ago!

2 pounds peeled, cubed sweet potatoes

1 cup unsweetened applesauce

1 egg yolk

1 teaspoon vanilla extract

1/2 teaspoon ground cinnamon

1/4 teaspoon ground allspice

2 egg whites

Cooking spray

1/2 cup firmly packed brown sugar

2 tablespoons all-purpose flour

1 teaspoon grated orange rind

1 tablespoon reduced-calorie margarine, melted

Cook sweet potatoes in boiling water 15 minutes or until tender; drain well and let cool. Position knife blade in food processor bowl. Add sweet potatoes and applesauce; process until smooth. Add egg yolk, vanilla extract, cinnamon, and allspice; process until smooth. Spoon into a bowl; set aside. Beat egg whites at room temperature until stiff peaks form. Gently stir one-third of egg whites into sweet potato mixture, then gently fold in remaining egg whites. Spoon into a 1 1/2 quart souffle dish coated with cooking spray. Combine brown sugar, flour, orange rind, and margarine; sprinkle over sweet potato mixture. Bake at 350° for 35 minutes or until knife inserted near the center comes out clean.

Preparation time: 25 minutes—Cooking time: 50 minutes

NUTRIENT INFORMATION

Servings per recipe: 11—Serving size: 1/2 cup

Protein 2 g, Carbohydrate 20 g, Fat 1 g, Saturated Fat <1 g,
Cholesterol 19 mg, Sodium 31 mg, Dietary Fiber 3 g

Calories 97
From protein: 8%; From carbohydrate: 82%; From fat: 9%

Food Exchanges: 1 starch, 1 vegetable

SWEET POTATOES
from the White House Cookbook, 1894

Boiled, steamed and baked the same as Irish potatoes; generally cooked with their jackets on. Cold sweet potatoes may be cut in slices across or lengthwise, and fried as common potatoes; or may be cut in half and served cold.

Boiled sweet potatoes are very nice. Boil until partly done, peel them and bake brown, basting them with butter or beef drippings several times. Served hot. They should be a nice brown.

BAKED SWEET POTATOES

from the White House Cookbook, 1894

Wash and scrape them, split them lengthwise. Steam or boil them until nearly done. Drain, and put them in a baking dish, placing over them lumps of butter, pepper and salt; sprinkle thickly with sugar, and bake in the oven to a nice brown.

Hubbard squash is nice cooked in the same manner.

✴TWICE-BAKED✴ SWEET POTATOES

*Use sweet potatoes as a vitamin A-rich substitute
for conventional baked potato side dishes.*

1 3/4 pounds small, unpeeled sweet potatoes

1/2 cup golden raisins

1/2 teaspoon brown sugar substitute

1/4 teaspoon ground cinnamon

1/4 teaspoon allspice

1/4 teaspoon nutmeg

8-ounce can unsweetened crushed pineapple, drained

2 tablespoons chopped pecans

1 cup miniature marshmallows

*P*lace potatoes on a baking sheet. Bake at 400° for 1 hour or until tender. Let cool 15 minutes. Cut each potato in half lengthwise; carefully scoop pulp into a bowl, leaving shells intact. Mash pulp; stir in raisins, brown sugar substitute, cinnamon, allspice, nutmeg, and pineapple. Spoon into shells; sprinkle with pecans and marshmallows. Bake at 400° for 15 minutes or until thoroughly heated.

*Preparation time: 15 minutes—Cooking time: 1 hour and 15 minutes
Cooling time: 15 minutes*

NUTRIENT INFORMATION

Servings per recipe: 8—Serving size: 1/2 potato

*Protein 1 g, Carbohydrate 18 g, Fat 1 g, Saturated Fat <1 g,
Cholesterol 0, Sodium 6 mg, Dietary Fiber 2 g*

*Calories 85
From protein: 5%; From carbohydrate: 85%; From fat: 11%*

Food Exchanges: 1 starch

⚜SOUTHERN-FRIED⚜ GREEN TOMATOES WITH CRUNCHY CORN SALSA

One hundred years ago, many people believed that tomatoes were poisonous or caused cancer. Today we eat them in quantities second only to the potato. Enjoy this delicious version of a classic Southern dish.

Salsa:

1/2 cup finely diced celery

1/2 cup finely diced green pepper

1/2 cup finely diced red bell pepper

2 teaspoons dried basil

2 tablespoons chopped jalapeno pepper, drained

1 clove garlic, minced

1 teaspoon olive oil

1 cup frozen white shoepeg corn, thawed

Tomatoes:

3 tablespoons yellow cornmeal

2 tablespoons grated Parmesan cheese

1/8 teaspoon salt

1/8 teaspoon black pepper

2 medium green tomatoes, cut into 1/4-inch thick slices

2 teaspoons olive oil

2 medium red tomatoes, cut into 1/4-inch thick slices

Combine all salsa ingredients in a bowl. Stir well. Cover and chill for 1 hour. Combine cornmeal and cheese in shallow dish. Sprinkle salt and pepper over green tomato slices and place slices, one at a time, into cornmeal mixture. Turn to coat.

FRIED AND BROILED TOMATOES
from the White House Cookbook, 1894

*C*ut firm, large, ripe tomatoes into thick slices, rather more than a quarter of an inch thick. Season with salt and pepper, dredge well with flour, or roll in egg and crumbs, and fry them brown on both sides evenly, in hot butter and lard mixed. Or, prepare them the same as for frying, broiling on a well-greased gridiron, seasoning afterward the same as beefsteak. A good accompaniment to steak. Or, having prepared the following sauce, a pint of milk, a tablespoonful of flour, and one beaten egg, salt, pepper and a very little mace; cream an ounce of butter, whisk into it the milk and let it simmer until it thickens; pour the sauce on a hot side-dish and arrange the tomatoes in the centre.

Heat olive oil in a large nonstick skillet over medium-high heat. Add green tomato slices and cook 3 minutes on each side or until browned. Arrange corn salsa, fried green tomato slices, and red tomato slices on a serving platter. Garnish with basil sprigs if desired. Serve immediately.

Preparation time: 10 minutes—Chilling time for salsa: 1 hour
Cooking time: 6 minutes

NUTRIENT INFORMATION

Servings per recipe: 4—Serving size: 1/2 cup salsa, 2 slices each of green and red tomatoes

Protein 5 g, Carbohydrate 24 g, Fat 5 g, Saturated Fat 1 g,
Cholesterol 2 mg, Sodium 233 mg, Dietary Fiber 4 g

Calories 161
From protein: 12%; From carbohydrate: 60%; From fat: 28%

Food Exchanges: 1 starch, 1 vegetable, 1 fat

VEGETABLE HASH

from the White House Cookbook, 1894

*C*hop rather coarsely the remains of vegetables left from
a boiled dinner, such as cabbage, parsnips, potatoes, etc.;
sprinkle over them a little pepper, place in a saucepan or frying pan
over the fire; put in a piece of butter the size of a hickory nut; when
it begins to melt, tip the dish so as to oil the bottom and around the
sides; then put in the chopped vegetables, pour in a spoonful or two
of hot water from the tea-kettle, and cover quickly so as to keep in the
steam. When heated thoroughly, take off the cover and stir occasionally until well cooked. Serve hot. Persons fond of vegetables will
relish this dish very much.

CONFETTI VEGETABLE TOSS

George Bush once said, "I do not like broccoli, and I haven't liked it since I was a little kid and my mother made me eat it. And I'm President of the United States, and I'm not going to eat any more broccoli."
We think even President Bush would love this recipe!

2 cups broccoli florets

2 cups cauliflower florets

2 cups thinly sliced carrots

1 1/2 tablespoons reduced-calorie margarine, melted

1 tablespoon lemon pepper seasoning

1/2 teaspoon garlic powder

1 teaspoon parsley

Steam broccoli, cauliflower, and carrots, covered for 5 minutes; set aside and keep warm. Combine margarine, lemon pepper, garlic powder, and parsley in a large bowl; stir well. Add vegetables and toss gently to coat.

Preparation time: 5 minutes—Cooking time: 5 minutes

NUTRIENT INFORMATION

Servings per recipe: 4—Serving size: 1 cup

Protein 3 g, Carbohydrate 12 g, Fat 2 g, Saturated Fat <1 g, Cholesterol 0, Sodium 96 mg, Dietary Fiber 4 g

Calories 78
From protein: 15%; From carbohydrate: 62%; From fat: 23%

Food Exchanges: 1 starch

★

$\mathcal{D}$ESSERTS

★

❋ G R A N D M A ' S   G O O F Y ❋ C A K E

A moist and easy cake for those who like homemade cakes without a lot of work.

Cake:

1 1/2 cups sifted all-purpose flour

3 tablespoons cocoa powder

1 teaspoon baking soda

1 cup sugar

1/2 teaspoon salt

5 tablespoons canola oil

1 tablespoon white vinegar

1 teaspoon vanilla extract

1 cup cold water

Cooking spray

Frosting:

1 1/2 ounces fat-free cream cheese

2 tablespoons reduced-fat margarine

1/2 teaspoon vanilla extract

1 cup sifted powdered sugar

In a large mixing bowl, stir together dry cake ingredients. Make a hole in the middle of the dry ingredients and pour in oil, vinegar, and vanilla. Mix well with an electric mixer. Add cold water and mix again. Pour batter into 9" x 9" pan coated with cooking spray. Bake at 350° for 30 minutes. Cool cake at least 60 minutes before frosting.

Frosting can be made while cake is cooling. In a large mixing bowl, beat together cream cheese, margarine, and vanilla until light and fluffy. Gradually add powdered sugar, beating until smooth. Spread over cooled cake. Refrigerate frosted cake.

Preparation time: 20 minutes—Baking time: 30 minutes
Standing time: 60 minutes

NUTRIENT INFORMATION

Servings per recipe: 9—Serving size: 1 slice (1/9 of cake)

Protein 3 g, Carbohydrate 51 g, Fat 9 g, Saturated Fat 1 g,
Cholesterol 0, Sodium 318 mg, Dietary Fiber 1 g

Calories 297
From protein: 4%; From carbohydrate: 69%; From fat: 27%

Food Exchanges: 1 starch, 2 fruit, 2 fat

Both recipes can be doubled to make a 9"x13" cake.

CHOCOLATE CAKE Nº 1

from the White House Cookbook, 1894

One cup of butter and two cups of sugar stirred to a cream, with the yolks of five eggs added after they have been well beaten. Then stir into that one cup of milk; beat the whites of two of the eggs to a stiff froth and add that also; now put in three cups and a half of sifted flour, two heaping teaspoonfuls of baking powder having been stirred into it. Bake in jelly-cake tins.

MIXTURE FOR FILLING—Take the remaining three whites of the eggs beaten very stiff, two cupfuls of sugar boiled to almost candy or until it becomes stringy or almost brittle; take it hot from the fire and pour it very slowly on the beaten whites of egg, beating quite fast; add one-half cake of grated chocolate, a teaspoonful of vanilla extract. Stir it all until cool, then spread between each cake and over the top and sides.
This, when well made, is the premium cake of its kind.

⁂ELECTION CAKE⁂

This savory, sweet treat is sure to get your vote!

Cake:

1 cup boiling water

1/2 cup liquid Butter Buds®

1/2 cup brown sugar

1 cup molasses

1 teaspoon vanilla extract

2 teaspoons baking soda

1/4 teaspoon salt

1 teaspoon ground cinnamon

1 teaspoon ground ginger

1 teaspoon ground cloves

2 1/2 cups all-purpose flour

1/4 cup liquid egg substitute

1/2 cup raisins

Cooking spray

Apple-Cranberry Topping:

2 (21-ounce) cans apple-cranberry pie filling

2 tablespoons cornstarch

1 1/2 cups light whipped topping

In a mixing bowl, combine water, Butter Buds, sugar, molasses, and vanilla. In a separate bowl, sift together dry ingredients; add to molasses mixture and mix well with an electric mixer. Beat in egg substitute. Stir in raisins. Pour batter into a 9" x 13" pan that has been coated with cooking spray. Bake at 350° for 30-35 minutes, or until a toothpick inserted into the center of the cake comes out clean.

While cake is baking, prepare apple-cranberry topping. In a medium pan, place pie filling and cornstarch. Stir until cornstarch is evenly dispersed throughout pie filling. Place pan over low heat and cook, stirring occasionally,

ELECTION CAKE
from the White House Cookbook, 1894

---

*T*hree cups milk, two cups sugar, one cup yeast; stir to a batter and let stand overnight; in the morning add two cups sugar, two cups butter, three eggs, half a nutmeg, one tablespoonful cinnamon, one pound raisins, a gill of brandy.

Brown sugar is much better than white for this kind of cake, and it is improved by dissolving a half-teaspoonful soda in a tablespoonful of milk in the morning. It should stand in the greased pans and rise some time until quite light for baking.

until topping is thickened—about 20 minutes. When cake is baked, spread with apple-cranberry topping. Allow to cool slightly, about 30 minutes, before serving. Top each piece with 1 tablespoon of light whipped topping.

Preparation time: 40 minutes (including time for preparing topping)
Baking time: 30-35 minutes—Standing time: 30 minutes

NUTRIENT INFORMATION

Servings per recipe: 24
Serving size: 1 slice cake and topping (1/24 of cake), 1 tablespoon whipped topping

Protein 2 g, Carbohydrate 41 g, Fat 1 g, Saturated Fat <1 g,
Cholesterol <1 mg, Sodium 220 mg, Dietary Fiber 1 g

Calories 181
From protein: 4%; From carbohydrate: 91%; From fat: 5%

Food Exchanges: 1 starch, 2 fruit

WHITE MOUNTAIN CAKE N$^{O.}$ 1

from the White House Cookbook, 1894

*T*wo cups of sugar, two-thirds cup of butter, the whites of seven eggs well beaten, two-thirds cup of sweet milk, two cups of flour, one cup of cornstarch, two teaspoonfuls baking powder. Bake in jelly cake tins.

FROSTING—Whites of three eggs and some sugar beaten together not quite as stiff as usual for frosting; spread over the cake, add some grated cocoanut, then put your cakes together; put cocoanut and frosting on top.

⁂NEW-FASHIONED⁂ WHITE MOUNTAIN CAKE

A time-consuming creation, yet the mountain of great taste is worth it! A special treat for a special occasion!

Cake:

1 cup reduced-fat stick margarine, softened

2 cups sugar

1 cup liquid egg substitute

3 cups sifted cake flour

1 tablespoon baking powder

1/4 teaspoon salt

1 cup skim milk

1 teaspoon vanilla extract

1 1/2 teaspoons almond extract

Cooking spray

Lemony Filling:

3 tablespoons cornstarch

6 tablespoons sugar

1/4 teaspoon salt

1 1/3 cups skim milk

2 tablespoons reduced-fat stick margarine

6 tablespoons freshly squeezed lemon juice

1 1/8 teaspoons grated lemon rind

Fat-Free Frosting:

1 1/2 cups sugar

Dash of salt

2 egg whites

5 tablespoons cold water

continued

N E W - F A S H I O N E D   W H I T E   M O U N T A I N   C A K E *(continued)*

1 tablespoon light corn syrup

1 teaspoon vanilla extract

1 1/2 cups shredded coconut

To make cake, first, cream margarine with an electric mixer. Slowly add sugar, beating well at medium speed. Add egg substitute, 1/4 cup at a time, beating well after each addition.

In a separate bowl, sift together flour, baking powder, and salt. Add to creamed mixture, alternately with skim milk, beginning and ending with flour mixture. Mix after each addition. Stir in vanilla and almond extracts last.

Pour batter into three 9" round cake pans coated with cooking spray and sprinkled with flour. Bake at 350° for 25-30 minutes, or until a toothpick inserted in center of cakes comes out clean. Cool cakes in pans 10 minutes, then turn out cakes to cool completely, approximately 1 1/2 hours.

While cakes are baking, prepare lemony filling. In a saucepan, combine cornstarch, sugar, and salt. Gradually whisk in milk until well blended. Add margarine and place saucepan over medium heat. Whisking constantly, bring to a boil and cook until thickened, approximately one minute. Remove pan from heat; stir in lemon juice and lemon rind. Pour filling into a container, cover, and chill until cakes are cooled.

When cakes are nearly cooled, prepare frosting. Combine all ingredients, except vanilla extract and coconut, in top of a large double boiler. Beat with an electric mixer at low speed for 30 seconds, or until just blended.

Place double boiler over boiling water; beat constantly on high speed for seven minutes, or until stiff peaks form. Remove double boiler from heat. Add vanilla extract and beat two minutes, or until frosting is thick enough to spread.

To assemble cake, spread the bottom layer with half of the lemony filling and sprinkle with 1/4 cup coconut. Repeat with second layer. Add third cake; frost top and sides of cake. Sprinkle top and sides with remaining one cup coconut. Refrigerate.

Preparation time: 55 minutes—Baking time: 25-30 minutes
Standing time: 1 hour 40 minutes

NUTRIENT INFORMATION

Servings per recipe: 12—Serving size: 1 slice (1/12 of cake)

Protein 7 g, Carbohydrate 98 g, Fat 14 g, Saturated Fat 5 g,
Cholesterol 1 mg, Sodium 533 mg, Dietary Fiber 1 g

Calories 546
From protein: 5%; From carbohydrate: 72%; From fat: 23%

Food Exchanges: 4 starch, 2 fruit, 2 fat

☙ CHOCOLATE CHERUB ❧ CAKE

A delightful creation for angel food cake lovers!
Very little fat, yet tastes sinful!

Cake:

1 1/2 cups egg whites

1/8 teaspoon salt

1 teaspoon cream of tartar

2 cups sugar

1/2 teaspoon lemon juice

1/2 teaspoon vanilla extract

1 cup all-purpose flour

1 teaspoon baking powder

1/2 cup cocoa powder

Cooking spray

Icing:

1 cup sifted powdered sugar

1/4 teaspoon vanilla extract

1 1/2 tablespoons skim milk

1 teaspoon cocoa powder

Filling:

1 1/2 cups instant vanilla pudding (made with skim milk)

1/3 cup mini milk chocolate chips

*B*eat the egg whites and salt until creamy. Add cream of tartar and beat until stiff peaks form. Fold in sugar, lemon juice, and vanilla. In a separate bowl, sift flour, baking powder, and cocoa two times, then fold into egg white mixture. Pour into tube pan lightly sprayed with cooking spray. Bake at 350° for 55-60 minutes. Remove from oven and turn out of pan immediately. Allow cake to cool at least 45 minutes before icing. In a mixing bowl stir together icing ingredients and drizzle over cooled cake.

ANGEL CAKE

from the White House Cookbook, 1894

Put into one tumbler of flour one teaspoonful of cream of tartar, then sift it five times. Sift also one glass and a half of white powdered sugar. Beat to a stiff froth the whites of eleven eggs; stir the sugar into the eggs by degrees, very lightly and carefully, adding three teaspoonfuls of vanilla extract. After this add the flour, stirring quickly and lightly. Pour it into a clean, bright tin cake-dish, which should not be buttered or lined. Bake at once in a moderate oven about forty minutes, testing it with a broom splint. When done let it remain in the cake-tin, turning it upside down, with the sides resting on the tops of two saucers so that a current of air will pass under and over it. This is the best recipe found after trying several. A perfection cake.

If a stuffed cake is desired, once cake has cooled and before it is iced, cut the top off the cake. Hollow out the inside of the cake bottom. Fill cake with a layer of pudding and a layer of chocolate chips. Replace top of cake and ice as directed above. Refrigerate.

Preparation time: 30 minutes—Baking time: 55-60 minutes
Standing time: 45 minutes

NUTRIENT INFORMATION

Servings per recipe: 14—Serving size: 1 slice (1/14 of cake) including filling

Protein 5 g, Carbohydrate 53 g, Fat 2 g, Saturated Fat <1 g,
Cholesterol 2 mg, Sodium 130 mg, Dietary Fiber <1 g

Calories 250
From protein: 8%; From carbohydrate: 85%; From fat: 7%

Food Exchanges: 3 starch

❊Light-as-a-Feather❊ Gingerbread

A rich-tasting, but light conclusion to a special dinner.

Gingerbread:

1/2 cup warm water

1/2 cup liquid Butter Buds®

1/2 cup packed light brown sugar

1/2 cup molasses

1/4 cup liquid egg substitute

1 1/2 cups all-purpose flour

1/4 teaspoon salt

1/2 teaspoon baking powder

1/2 teaspoon baking soda

3/4 teaspoon ground ginger

3/4 teaspoon ground cinnamon

Cooking spray

Caramel Sauce:

1/2 cup liquid egg substitute

1 cup evaporated skim milk

2 cups packed light brown sugar

1 tablespoon all-purpose flour

3 tablespoons skim milk

2 tablespoons liquid Butter Buds

In a large mixing bowl, combine water and Butter Buds. Add sugar, molasses, and egg substitute and beat well with an electric mixer. Sift together dry ingredients and add to wet ingredients. Beat until smooth. Pour into 8" x 8" pan that has been coated with cooking spray and sprinkled with flour. Bake at 350° for 25-30 minutes. Cool in pan 30 minutes before cutting.

Caramel sauce can be made while gingerbread is baking. Combine egg substitute, evaporated skim milk, and sugar in top of double boiler; mix

SOFT GINGER CAKE
from the White House Cookbook, 1894

Stir to a cream one cupful of butter and half a cupful of brown sugar; add to this two cupfuls of cooking molasses; a cupful of sweet milk, a tablespoonful of ginger, a teaspoonful of ground cinnamon; beat all thoroughly together, then add three eggs, the whites and yolks beaten separately; beat into this two cups of sifted flour, then a teaspoonful of soda dissolved in a spoonful of water and last, two more cupfuls of sifted flour. Butter and paper two common square breadpans, divide the mixture and pour half into each. Bake in a moderate oven. This cake requires long and slow baking, from forty to sixty minutes. I find that if sour milk is used the cakes are much lighter, but either sweet or sour is most excellent.

well. Dissolve flour in the 3 tablespoons skim milk. Add slowly to sugar mixture, whisking well with wire whisk after each addition. Whisking constantly, cook until creamy. Whisk in Butter Buds and remove from heat. Serve while warm over gingerbread. Gingerbread recipe can be doubled to make 9" x 13" pan.

Preparation time: 25 minutes—Baking time: 25-30 minutes
Standing time: 30 minutes

NUTRIENT INFORMATION

Servings per recipe: 9 gingerbread, 10 caramel sauce
Serving size: 1 slice cake (1/9 of cake), 1/4 cup caramel sauce

Protein 7 g, Carbohydrate 87 g, Fat 1 g, Saturated Fat <1 g,
Cholesterol 1 mg, Sodium 442 mg, Dietary Fiber 1 g

Calories 385
From protein: 7%; From carbohydrate: 90%; From fat: 2%

Food Exchanges: 3 starch, 3 fruit

❋ SWEET STRAWBERRY ❋ MERINGUE CAKE

A beautiful and luscious finale!

Cake:

1 box light yellow cake mix

1 cup orange juice

1/3 cup water

2 egg yolks

1/2 cup liquid egg substitute

1 teaspoon grated orange peel

Cooking spray

2 tablespoons flour

Meringue:

4 egg whites

1/4 teaspoon cream of tartar

1 cup sugar

Topping:

4 cups light whipped topping

1 quart fresh strawberries

Combine first six ingredients in a large mixing bowl. Beat with an electric mixer for 4 minutes. Pour batter into two 9" cake pans that have been coated with cooking spray and sprinkled with the 2 tablespoons flour. Before baking, top each pan with meringue.

To make meringue, first whip egg whites until frothy with an electric mixer. Add cream of tartar to egg whites and whip until stiff, but not dry. Egg whites should stand in peaks that lean over slightly when the beaters are removed. Beat in sugar, 1/4 cup at a time. Spread meringue over the two pans of batter. Bake cakes at 350° for 35-40 minutes.

S W E E T   S T R A W B E R R Y   C A K E

from the White House Cookbook, 1894

*T*hree eggs, one cupful of sugar, two of flour, one tablespoonful of butter, a teaspoonful, heaped, of baking powder. Beat the butter and sugar together and add the eggs well beaten. Stir in the flour and baking powder well sifted together. Bake in deep tin plate. This quantity will fill four plates. With three pints of strawberries mix a cupful of sugar and mash them a little. Spread the fruit between the layers of cake. The top layer of strawberries may be covered with a meringue made with the white of an egg and a tablespoonful of powdered sugar. Save out the largest berries and arrange them around in circles on the top in the white frosting. Makes a very fancy dish, as well as a most delicious cake.

Place cake pans on rack to cool. Cool cakes completely in pans—at least 2 hours. Turn cakes out of pans and immediately place meringue-side up. Spread 2/3 of whipped topping over bottom layer. Slice 3/4 of the berries and place over whipped topping. Add top layer and spread with remaining whipped topping. Arrange whole berries on whipped topping. Keep refrigerated.

Preparation time: 35 minutes—Baking time: 35-40 minutes
Cooling time: 2 hours

N U T R I E N T   I N F O R M A T I O N

Servings per recipe: 14—Serving size: 1 slice (1/14 of cake)

Protein 4 g, Carbohydrate 56 g, Fat 7 g, Saturated Fat 1 g,
Cholesterol 30 mg, Sodium 294 mg, Dietary Fiber 1 g

Calories 303
From protein: 5%; From carbohydrate: 74%; From fat: 21%

Food Exchanges: 2 starch, 2 fruit, 1 fat

⁂ CLASSIC ⁂ GINGERSNAPS

A classic treat. For a variation that children love, cut large marshmallows in half and place a marshmallow half, cut-side down, on each cookie during last four minutes of baking.

1 1/4 sticks reduced-fat margarine

1 cup packed light brown sugar

1/4 cup molasses

1/4 cup liquid egg substitute

2 1/4 cups sifted all-purpose flour

2 teaspoons baking soda

1/2 teaspoon salt

1 teaspoon ground ginger

1 teaspoon ground cinnamon

1/2 teaspoon ground cloves

1/4 cup sugar

Cooking spray

*P*lace first four ingredients in a large mixing bowl and cream together using an electric mixer. Beat until fluffy. In a separate bowl, sift together flour, baking soda, salt, ginger, cinnamon, and cloves. Stir into molasses mixture. Chill dough 1 hour.

Place remaining 1/4 cup sugar in a small bowl. Form dough into 3/4 inch balls and roll in sugar. Place balls 2 inches apart on a baking sheet coated with cooking spray. Bake at 375° for 12 minutes. May be eaten warm or placed on a wire cooling rack to cool.

Preparation time: 40 minutes—Chilling time: 60 minutes
Baking time: 12 minutes per pan

NUTRIENT INFORMATION

Servings per recipe: 48—Serving size: 1 cookie

Protein 1 g, Carbohydrate 11 g, Fat 1 g, Saturated Fat <1 g,
Cholesterol <1 mg, Sodium 106 mg, Dietary Fiber <1 g

Calories 57
From protein: 7%; From carbohydrate: 77%; From fat: 16%

Food Exchanges: 1 starch

BAKERS' GINGER SNAPS

from the White House Cookbook, 1894

Boil all together the following ingredients: Two cups of brown sugar, two cups of cooking molasses, one cup of shortening, which should be part butter, one large tablespoonful of ginger; one tablespoonful of ground cinnamon, one teaspoonful of cloves; remove from the fire and let it cool. In the meantime, sift four cups of flour and stir part of it into the above mixture. Now dissolve a teaspoonful of soda in a tablespoonful of warm water and beat into this mixture, stir in the remainder of flour and make stiff enough to roll into long rolls about an inch in diameter, and cut off from the end into half-inch pieces. Place them on well-buttered tins, giving plenty of room to spread. Bake in a moderate oven. Let them cool before taking out of the tins.

❊Gingersnap❊ Pumpkin Pie

"Hurrah for the fun! Is the turkey done? Hurrah for the pumpkin pie!"
—Lydia Maria Clark

Crust:

1 3/4 cups gingersnap crumbs

3 tablespoons reduced-fat margarine, melted

Cooking spray

Filling:

15-ounce can pumpkin

1/2 cup liquid egg substitute

14-ounce can fat-free sweetened condensed milk

1 teaspoon vanilla extract

1/4 teaspoon salt

1/2 teaspoon ground ginger

1 teaspoon ground cinnamon

1/2 teaspoon ground nutmeg

In a mixing bowl, stir together crumbs and margarine. Press firmly into 9" pie plate coated with cooking spray. Set aside. In a large mixing bowl, combine filling ingredients. Mix well and pour into crust. Cover edges of crust with foil to prevent burning. Bake at 425° for 10 minutes. Reduce oven temperature to 350° and bake 40-45 minutes longer, or until a knife inserted 1 inch from edge of pie comes out clean. Cool before slicing. Refrigerate leftovers.

Note: If desired, a refrigerated pastry crust may be used instead of the gingersnap crust. The pastry crust, however, would increase the fat, saturated fat, and cholesterol content of the pie.

Preparation time: 25 minutes—Baking time: 50-55 minutes

N U T R I E N T   I N F O R M A T I O N

Servings per recipe: 8—Serving size: 1 slice (1/8 of pie)

Protein 8 g, Carbohydrate 55 g, Fat 5 g, Saturated Fat 1 g,
Cholesterol <1 mg, Sodium 357 mg, Dietary Fiber 2 g

Calories 297
From protein: 11%; From carbohydrate: 74%; From fat: 15%

Food Exchanges: 1 starch, 2 fruit, 1 low-fat milk

PUMPKIN PIE N$^{O.}$ 1
from the White House Cookbook, 1894

For three pies: One quart of milk, three cupfuls of boiled and strained pumpkin, one and one-half cupfuls of sugar, one-half cupful of molasses, the yolks and whites of four eggs beaten separately, a little salt, one tablespoonful each of ginger and cinnamon. Beat all together and bake with an under crust. Boston marrow or Hubbard squash may be substituted for pumpkin and are much preferred by many, as possessing a less strong flavor.

❊MODERN-DAY❊ MAIDS OF HONOR

*Maids of Honor were the ideal dessert during winters
in colonial times because they did not require fresh fruit.
The origin of their name remains a mystery.*

Lemon Custard Filling:

3/4 cup sugar

3 tablespoons cornstarch

1 1/2 cups nonfat buttermilk

1 1/2 tablespoons reduced-fat stick margarine

3/4 cup liquid egg substitute

1 1/2 teaspoons grated lemon rind

1/4 cup lemon juice concentrate

Tart Shells:

3 ounces fat-free cream cheese

1 cup all-purpose flour

6 tablespoons reduced-fat stick margarine

Cooking spray

Prepare filling first. Combine sugar and cornstarch in a saucepan. Add buttermilk, stirring well. Cook over low heat, stirring constantly, until thickened. Stir in margarine. Remove from heat.

In a bowl, mix together remaining filling ingredients. Gradually add about one-fourth of hot mixture to egg mixture, whisking constantly. Add this back into pan of hot mixture, again whisking constantly. Return pan to stove and cook over low heat, whisking continually, for 4 minutes or until smooth and thickened. Cover and chill 1 1/2 hours.

Prepare tart shells while filling is chilling. Combine all 3 ingredients in a mixing bowl. Beat with an electric mixer until blended. Use hands to knead dough into a ball. Divide the dough into 12 equal portions. Coat muffin

M A I D S   O F   H O N O R

from the White House Cookbook, 1894

*T*ake one cupful of sour milk, one of sweet milk, a tablespoonful of
melted butter, the yolks of four eggs, juice and rind of one lemon
and a small cupful of white pounded sugar. Put both kinds of milk
together in a vessel, which is set in another and let it become sufficiently heated to set the curd, then strain off the milk, rub the curd through
a strainer, add butter to the curd, the sugar, well-beaten eggs and
lemon. Line the little pans with the riches of puff paste and fill with
the mixture; bake until firm in the centre, from ten to fifteen minutes.

tins with cooking spray. Line each muffin cup with a portion of dough by
pressing the dough with your fingers to coat the entire cup. Bake at 350°
for 12-13 minutes, or until golden. Cool 5 minutes in muffin tins,
then turn shells out to finish cooling.

Fill each tart shell with lemon custard. May garnish each tart
with a whole strawberry. Best if served immediately.

Preparation time: 40 minutes—Chilling time: 1 hour 30 minutes
Baking time: 12-13 minutes

N U T R I E N T   I N F O R M A T I O N

Servings per recipe: 12—Serving size: 1 tart

Protein 5 g, Carbohydrate 25 g, Fat 4 g, Saturated Fat 1 g,
Cholesterol 1 mg, Sodium 185 mg, Dietary Fiber <1 g

Calories 156
From protein: 13%; From carbohydrate: 64%; From fat: 23%

Food Exchanges: 1 starch, 1 skim milk

❅ S N O W B A L L S ❅ AND CUSTARD

A light dessert for a summer dinner party on the patio.

Meringues:

1/8 teaspoon cream of tartar

2 egg whites

3/4 cup sugar

Custard Sauce:

1/2 cup liquid egg substitute

1/2 cup sugar

2 1/2 cups skim milk

2 teaspoons vanilla extract

2 cups sliced strawberries (may sweeten if desired)

To prepare meringues, combine cream of tartar and egg whites in a mixing bowl; beat with an electric mixer until soft peaks form. Gradually add sugar and continue to beat until stiff peaks form. Spoon meringue into 4 circles on a baking sheet lined with brown paper (a new brown lunch sack that is cut open works well). Using a spoon, form a depression in the center of each meringue circle. Once baked, these will serve as meringue shells. Bake at 275° for one hour then turn oven off and leave meringues in oven for 2 hours to dry out. Remove from papered baking sheet after cooled.

While meringues are drying, prepare custard sauce. Combine egg substitute and sugar in a large saucepan; gradually stir in milk. Cook over medium heat, whisking constantly, until custard thickens about 20 minutes). Remove from heat and stir in vanilla extract. Cover and chill until ready to use. If desired, may thin with additional skim milk.

To assemble dessert, pour 3/4 cup custard in each serving dish. Place meringue on top of custard and fill each meringue shell with 1/2 cup strawberries.

Preparation time: 50 minutes
Baking time: 3 hours (including drying time for meringues)

NUTRIENT INFORMATION

Servings per recipe: 4—Serving size: 1 meringue, 3/4 cup custard, 1/2 cup strawberries

Protein 11 g, Carbohydrate 76 g, Fat 2 g, Saturated Fat <1 g,
Cholesterol 3 mg, Sodium 161 mg, Dietary Fiber 1 g

Calories 366
From protein: 12%; From carbohydrate: 83%; From fat: 5%

Food Exchanges: 4 starch, 1 fruit

SNOWBALL CUSTARD

from the White House Cookbook, 1894

Soak half a package of Cox's gelatine in a teacupful of cold water one hour, to which add a pint of boiling water, stir it until the gelatine is thoroughly dissolved. Then beat the whites of four eggs to a stiff froth, put two teacupfuls of sugar in the gelatine water first, then the beaten white of egg and one teaspoonful of vanilla extract, or the grated rind and the juice of a lemon. Whip it some time until it is all quite stiff and cold. Dip some teacups or wine-glasses in cold water and fill them; set in a cold place.

In the meantime, make a boiled custard of the yolks of three of the eggs, with half a cupful of sugar and a pint of milk; flavor with vanilla extract. Now after the meringue in the cups has stood four or five hours, turn them out of the molds, place them in a glass dish and pour this custard around the base.

⚜ RASPBERRY-PEACH ⚜ TRIFLE

Prepare this dessert early in the day, then go play!
The flavor improves with time.

16-ounce package unsweetened frozen peach slices, thawed

12-ounce package unsweetened frozen raspberries, thawed

2 tablespoons sugar

3 1/2-ounce box instant vanilla pudding

1 3/4 cups skim milk

12-ounce container light whipped topping

13 1/2-ounce commercial fat-free pound cake loaf, cut into 1" cubes

1/2 cup orange juice

*I*n a large bowl, combine peaches, raspberries, and sugar. Toss to coat and set aside. In a mixing bowl, combine pudding mix and skim milk. With a wire whisk, mix 1-2 minutes or until well blended. Place pudding in refrigerator for 5 minutes, or until soft-set. Fold in half of whipped topping.

Place half of cake in bottom of trifle bowl and drizzle with half of orange juice. Arrange half of fruit over cake and top with half of pudding mixture. Repeat layers. Cover and chill at least two hours. If desired, spread remaining whipped topping over trifle before serving.

Preparation time: 30 minutes—Chilling time: 2 hours

NUTRIENT INFORMATION

Servings per recipe: 16—Serving size: 1 cup

Protein 3 g, Carbohydrate 49 g, Fat 3 g, Saturated Fat <1 g, Cholesterol 1 mg, Sodium 472 mg, Dietary Fiber 2 g

Calories 235
From protein: 5%; From carbohydrate: 83%; From fat: 11%

Food Exchanges: 1 starch, 2 fruit, 1 fat

FRUIT TRIFLE

from the White House Cookbook, 1894

Whites of four eggs beaten to a stiff froth, two tablespoonfuls each of sugar, currant jelly and raspberry jam. Eaten with sponge cakes, it is a delicious dessert.

MERINGUES
OR KISSES
from the White House Cookbook, 1894

A coffeecupful of fine white sugar, the whites of six eggs; whisk the whites of the eggs to a stiff froth and with a wooden spoon stir in quickly the pounded sugar; and have some boards put in the oven thick enough to prevent the bottom of the meringues from acquiring too much color. Cut some strips of paper about two inches wide; place this paper on the board and drop a tablespoonful at a time of the mixture on the paper, taking care to let all the meringues be the same size. In dropping it from the spoon, give the mixture the form of an egg and keep the meringues about two inches apart from each other on the paper. Strew over them some sifted sugar and bake in a moderate oven for half an hour. As soon as they begin to color, remove them from the oven; take each slip of paper by the two ends and turn it gently on the table and with a small spoon take out the soft part of each meringue. Spread some clean paper on the board, turn the meringues upside down and put them into the oven to harden and brown on the other side. When required for table, fill them with whipped cream, flavored with liquor or vanilla and sweeten with pounded sugar. Join two of the meringues together and pile them high in the dish. To vary their appearance, finely chopped almonds or currants may be strewn over them before the sugar is sprinkled over, and they may be garnished with any bright-colored preserve. Great expedition is necessary in making this sweet dish, as, if the meringues are not put into the oven as soon as the sugar and eggs are mixed, the former melts and the mixture would run on the paper instead of keeping its egg-shape. The sweeter the meringues are made the crisper they will be; but if there is not sufficient sugar mixed with them, they will most likely be tough. They are sometimes colored with cochineal; and if kept well covered in a dry place, will remain good for a month or six weeks.

⊰JUDY'S FRUIT KISSES⊱

Looking for a fat-free cookie that tastes great? This is it!

3 egg whites

1/8 teaspoon salt

1/8 teaspoon cream of tartar

1 teaspoon vanilla extract

3/4 cup sugar

3/4 cup diced candied fruit

Combine first four ingredients in a large bowl; beat with an electric mixer until soft peaks form. Gradually beat in sugar and continue to beat until stiff peaks form. Fold in fruit. Drop by teaspoonfuls onto cookie sheet lined with brown paper (a new brown lunch sack that is cut open works well).

Bake at 275° for 1 hour, or until meringues are crisp and dried out. Turn oven off and leave in closed oven to cool. Remove from papered pan after cooled.

Preparation time: 20 minutes—Baking time: 1 hour

NUTRIENT INFORMATION

Servings per recipe: 30—Serving size: 1 cookie

Protein <1 g, Carbohydrate 9 g, Fat 0, Saturated Fat 0, Cholesterol 0, Sodium 14 mg, Dietary Fiber <1 g

Calories 40
From protein: 10%; From carbohydrate: 90%; From fat: 0%

Food Exchanges: 1/2 starch

⁂QUICK CHOCOLATE⁂ CAKE-MIX COOKIES

These can be whipped up in no time if unexpected company arrives on your doorstep. The applesauce replaces part of the fat in this sweet treat.

18 1/4-ounce box light devil's food cake mix

1/2 cup liquid egg substitute

1/4 cup canola oil

1/4 cup unsweetened applesauce

Cooking spray

1/2 can low-fat chocolate frosting

*I*n a mixing bowl, combine the first four ingredients; stir until well blended. Drop by teaspoonfuls onto cookie sheet coated with cooking spray. Bake at 350° for 10-12 minutes. Cool on cooling rack and frost with chocolate frosting.

For variation you may want to stir chopped maraschino cherries or 1 tsp. grated orange rind into cookie dough. Another tasty and no-fat tip is to top each cookie with a thumbprint of strawberry jam instead of frosting.

Preparation time: 10 minutes—Baking time: 10-12 minutes per pan
Cooling time: 20 minutes

NUTRIENT INFORMATION

Servings per recipe: 30—Serving size: 1 cookie

Protein 2 g, Carbohydrate 20 g, Fat 4 g, Saturated Fat 1 g,
Cholesterol <1 mg, Sodium 152 mg, Dietary Fiber <1 g

Calories 124
From protein: 6%; From carbohydrate: 65%; From fat: 29%

Food Exchanges: 1 starch, 1 fat

CHOCOLATE MACAROONS
from the White House Cookbook, 1894

*P*ut three ounces of plain chocolate in a pan and melt on a slow fire; then work it to a thick paste with one pound of powdered sugar and the whites of three eggs; roll the mixture down to the thickness of about one-quarter of an inch; cut it in small, round pieces with a paste-cutter, either plain or scalloped; butter a pan slightly, and dust it with flour and sugar in equal quantities; place in it the pieces of paste or mixture, and bake in a hot, but not too quick oven.

RASPBERRY SHERBET

from the White House Cookbook, 1894

Two quarts of raspberries, one cupful of sugar, one pint and a half of water, the juice of a large lemon, one tablespoonful of gelatine. Mash the berries and sugar together and let them stand two hours. Soak the gelatine in cold water to cover. Add one pint of the water to the berries and strain. Dissolve the gelatine in half a pint of boiling water; add this to the strained mixture and freeze.

❄HOMEMADE❄
RASPBERRY SHERBET

Our Blueberry Teacakes are a nice complement.

3 (12-ounce) packages frozen,
unsweetened raspberries, thawed
1/4 cup orange juice
1/2 cup sugar
1 tablespoon lemon juice

Combine all ingredients in a blender and process until liquefied. Pour mixture through a wire-mesh strainer, pressing the back of a spoon against the strainer to squeeze out the juice. Discard seeds and pulp remaining in strainer. Pour juice mixture into an 8" x 8" square pan and freeze until almost firm, about 1 1/2 hours.

Spoon mixture into a mixing bowl and beat at medium speed with an electric mixer until mixture lightens in color. Return mixture to pan and freeze until firm, about 3 hours. To serve, let soften at room temperature for 10 minutes. Garnish with mint leaves.

Preparation time: 20 minutes—Freezing time: 4 1/2 hours
Standing time: 10 minutes

NUTRIENT INFORMATION

Servings per recipe: 8—Serving size: 1/2 cup

Protein 1 g, Carbohydrate 21 g, Fat <1 g, Saturated Fat <1 g,
Cholesterol 0, Sodium 2 mg, Dietary Fiber 1 g

Calories 93
From protein: 4%; From carbohydrate: 90%; From fat: 5%

Food Exchanges: 1 fruit, 1 fat

PLAIN BREAD PUDDING, BAKED

from the White House Cookbook, 1894

Break up about a pint of stale bread after cutting off the crust; pour over it a quart of boiling milk; add to this a piece of butter the size of a small egg; cover the dish tight and let it stand until cool; then with a spoon mash it until fine, adding a teaspoonful of cinnamon and one of nutmeg grated, half a cupful of sugar and one-quarter of a teaspoonful of soda dissolved in a little hot water. Beat up four eggs very light and add last. Turn all into a well-buttered pudding-dish and bake three-quarters of an hour. Serve it warm with hard sauce. This recipe may be steamed or boiled; very nice either way

✢ Biscuit Pudding ✢

Serve warm with our Kentucky Bourbon Sauce (recipe follows).

Biscuits:

2 cups baking mix

3/4 cup skim milk

Pudding:

10 biscuits

1 quart skim milk

1 1/2 cups liquid egg substitute

2 cups sugar

2 tablespoons vanilla extract

Cooking spray

2 tablespoons liquid Butter Buds®

To prepare biscuits, combine baking mix and skim milk in a large mixing bowl. Stir until ingredients are just mixed. Drop dough by spoonfuls onto an ungreased baking sheet to make 10 biscuits. Bake at 450° for 9 minutes, or until golden. After biscuits are baked and cooled, break them into small pieces and place in a large bowl. Add milk and allow biscuits to soak 5 minutes. Meanwhile, in a separate bowl, beat egg substitute with sugar and vanilla extract; add to biscuit mixture. Coat a 2-quart baking dish with cooking spray. Pour Butter Buds into bottom of baking dish; then add biscuit pudding. Bake at 350° for 45 minutes, or until set. Serve warm with Kentucky Bourbon Sauce.

Preparation time: 30 minutes
Baking time: 55 minutes (including baking time for biscuits)

N U T R I E N T   I N F O R M A T I O N

Servings per recipe: 10—Serving size: 3/4 cup

Protein 9 g, Carbohydrate 53 g, Fat 3 g, Saturated Fat 1 g, Cholesterol 2 mg, Sodium 283 mg, Dietary Fiber <1 g

Calories 275
From protein: 13%; From carbohydrate: 77%; From fat: 10%

Food Exchanges: 2 starch, 2 fruit

BRANDY OR WINE SAUCE N^{O.} 1

from the White House Cookbook, 1894

Stir a heaping teaspoonful of cornstarch in a little cold water to a smooth paste (or instead use a tablespoonful of sifted flour); add to it a cupful of boiling water, with one cupful of sugar, a piece of butter as large as an egg, and boil all together ten minutes. Remove from the fire and when cool, stir into it half a cupful of brandy or wine. It should be about as thick as thin syrup.

⸆KENTUCKY⸅ BOURBON SAUCE

Can be served warm over vanilla frozen yogurt,
as well as over our Biscuit Pudding.

1 cup sugar

1 cup evaporated skim milk

1/8 teaspoon ground cinnamon

1 tablespoon liquid Butter Buds®

1 tablespoon cornstarch

1/4 cup water

1 tablespoon bourbon

Combine first 4 ingredients in a saucepan. Cook over medium heat until sugar dissolves while whisking constantly with a wire whisk. In a small bowl, combine cornstarch and water; whisk into cream mixture and bring to a boil, whisking constantly. Boil one minute while continuing to whisk. Remove from heat and stir in bourbon.
Serve warm over our Biscuit Pudding.

Preparation time: 15 minutes

NUTRIENT INFORMATION

Servings per recipe: 10—Serving size: 1/8 cup

Protein 2 g, Carbohydrate 24 g, Fat <1 g, Saturated Fat <1 g,
Cholesterol 1 mg, Sodium 48 mg, Dietary Fiber <1 g

Calories 108
From protein: 7%; From carbohydrate: 89%; From fat: 0%; From alcohol: 4%

Food Exchanges: 1 starch

❊Banana Pudding❊ Surprise

Your taste buds won't let you believe this is low fat!
What a delightful surprise you'll find the chocolate syrup to be!

14-ounce can fat-free sweetened condensed milk

1 1/2 cups cold water

3 1/2-ounce box instant vanilla pudding

8 ounces fat-free sour cream

2 cups light whipped topping

45 vanilla wafers

3 large bananas

3/4 cup plus 2 tablespoons fat-free chocolate syrup

*I*n a large bowl, combine condensed milk and water; mix well. Add pudding mix and beat with an electric mixer until well blended. Chill 5 minutes then stir in sour cream. Fold in whipped topping. Cover bottom of a 2-quart dish with 15 vanilla wafers. Slice one banana over the vanilla wafers. Top with 1/4 cup chocolate syrup and 1/3 of the pudding. Repeat layering of vanilla wafers, banana, syrup, and pudding two more times. End with the pudding. Drizzle remaining 2 tablespoons chocolate syrup over top and swirl with a knife. Chill 3 hours. Keep refrigerated.

Preparation time: 35 minutes—Chilling time: 3 hours

NUTRIENT INFORMATION

Servings per recipe: 12—Serving size: 3/4 cup

Protein 6 g, Carbohydrate 62 g, Fat 4 g, Saturated Fat 1 g,
Cholesterol 10 mg, Sodium 234 mg, Dietary Fiber 1 g

Calories 308
From protein: 8%; From carbohydrate: 81%; From fat: 12%

Food Exchanges: 2 starch, 2 fruit, 1 fat

BANANA PUDDING

from the White House Cookbook, 1894

*C*ut sponge cake in slices, and, in a glass dish put alternately a layer of sponge cake and a layer of bananas sliced. Make a soft custard, flavor with a little wine, and pour over it. Beat the whites of the eggs to a stiff froth and heap over the whole.

Peaches cut up, left a few hours in sugar and then scalded, and added when cold to thick boiled custard, made rather sweet, are a delicious dessert.

❊ PEACH GENEVA ❊ WAFERS

A time-consuming, but splendid creation!

12-ounce jar peach preserves

1/4 teaspoon ground nutmeg

1/4 teaspoon ground cinnamon

1/4 teaspoon ground cloves

1 1/2 sticks reduced-fat margarine

8-ounce package fat-free cream cheese

2 tablespoons sugar

2 cups all-purpose flour

1 egg white, lightly beaten

2 teaspoons water

Cooking spray

1/4 cup sifted powdered sugar

For peach filling, combine first 4 ingredients in a small bowl and set aside. In a mixing bowl, beat margarine and cream cheese with an electric mixer until creamy; add sugar, beating well. Add flour, mixing on low speed until well blended. Cover dough and chill for 1 1/2 hours.

Divide dough into three portions; roll each portion to 1/16-inch thickness on a lightly floured surface, and cut with a 3-inch round cookie cutter. Spoon 1/2 teaspoon peach filling in center of each round. Combine egg and water in a small bowl; brush on opposite edges around preserves. Fold opposite sides to center, slightly overlapping edges; pinch to seal. Place on a baking sheet lightly coated with cooking spray.

Bake at 350° for 13 minutes, or until golden. Remove from baking sheet and place on wire rack to cool. Right before serving, sprinkle each with sifted powdered sugar.

Preparation time: 50 minutes—Chilling time: 1 hour 30 minutes
Baking time: 13 minutes—Cooling time: 20 minutes

N U T R I E N T   I N F O R M A T I O N

Servings per recipe: 36—Serving size: 1 cookie

Protein 2 g, Carbohydrate 13 g, Fat 2 g, Saturated Fat <1 g,
Cholesterol 0, Sodium 84 mg, Dietary Fiber <1 g

Calories 78
From protein: 10%; From carbohydrate: 67%; From fat: 23%

Food Exchanges: 1 starch

G E N E V A   W A F E R S

from the White House Cookbook, 1894

Two eggs, three ounces of butter, three ounces of flour, three
ounces of pounded sugar. Well whisk the eggs, put them into
a basin and stir to them the butter, which should be beaten to a
cream; add the flour and sifted sugar gradually, and then mix all well
together. Butter a baking sheet, and drop on it a teaspoonful of the
mixture at a time, leaving a space between each. Bake in a cool oven;
watch the pieces of paste, and when half done, roll them up like
wafers and put in a small wedge of bread or a piece of wood, to keep
them in shape. Return them to the oven until crisp. Before serving,
remove the bread, put a spoonful of preserve in the widest end, and
fill up with whipped cream. This is a very pretty and ornamental dish
for the supper-table, and is very nice and very easily made.

GRILLED ALMONDS

from the White House Cookbook, 1894

These are a very delicious candy seldom met with out of France. They are more trouble to make than other kinds, but well repay it from their novel flavor. Blanch a cupful of almonds; dry them thoroughly. Boil a cupful of sugar and a quarter of a cupful of water till it "hairs," then throw in the almonds; let them fry, as it were, in this syrup, stirring them occasionally; they will turn a faint yellow brown before the sugar changes color; do not wait an instant once this change of color begins, or they will lose flavor; remove them from the fire, and stir them until the syrup has turned back to sugar and clings irregularly to the nuts.

❋ SUGAR 'N SPICE ❋ ALMONDS

Makes a nice gift for the holiday season.

4 cups sugar, divided

1 1/2 teaspoons ground cinnamon, divided

1/2 cup water

1 pound whole almonds, shelled

*I*n a bowl, stir together 2 cups sugar and 3/4 teaspoon cinnamon. Pour onto a baking sheet and spread to cover sheet. Set aside. In a large saucepan bring 2 cups sugar, 3/4 teaspoon cinnamon, and water to a boil. Boil until the syrup spins a thread. Add almonds and stir to coat; keep pan over medium heat until all almonds are coated and the syrup returns to sugar. Pour almonds onto the baking sheet that has been coated with sugar and cinnamon. Toss almonds to coat. Separate almonds that become stuck together. Allow to cool, approximately 30 minutes, before storing in covered container.

Preparation time: 30 minutes—Cooling time: 30 minutes

NUTRIENT INFORMATION

Servings per recipe: 16—Serving size: 1 ounce (about 22 almonds)

Protein 7 g, Carbohydrate 55 g, Fat 13 g, Saturated Fat 1 g, Cholesterol 0, Sodium 1 mg, Dietary Fiber 2 g

Calories 365

From protein: 8%; From carbohydrate: 60%; From fat: 32%

Food Exchanges: 3 starch, 3 fat

❊Popcorn Snowballs❊

"Today, millions of Americans who sit munching popcorn before flickering movie screens, television sets, and fireplaces are following an ancient tradition. Throughout much of the hemisphere, generations of Indians popped corn in earthen vessels and ate it around open fires. One thousand-year-old specimens of the grain from ancient, musty Peruvian tombs still popped when heated!"
—Nicholas P. Hardeman

Enjoy a new rendition of this age-old treat!

16-ounce bag marshmallows

1/4 cup reduced-fat stick margarine

1 teaspoon vanilla extract

5 quarts air-popped popcorn

Cooking spray

In a large stock pot or Dutch oven, combine marshmallows and margarine. Cook over low heat, stirring occasionally, until marshmallows are melted. Stir in vanilla. Add popcorn 1 quart at a time and toss to coat after each addition. Coat hands with cooking spray and shape mixture into balls. Place balls on wax paper to cool. After cooling, wrap each popcorn ball in plastic wrap to store.

Preparation time: 30 minutes—Cooling time: 20 minutes

Nutrient Information

Servings per recipe: 15—Serving size: 1 ball

Protein 2 g, Carbohydrate 31 g, Fat 2 g, Saturated Fat <1 g, Cholesterol 0, Sodium 46 mg, Dietary Fiber 1 g

Calories 150
From protein: 5%; From carbohydrate: 83%; From fat: 12%

Food Exchanges: 2 starch

POP-CORN BALLS

from the White House Cookbook, 1894

Take three large ears of pop-corn (rice is best). After popping shake it down in pan so the unpopped corn will settle at the bottom; put the nice white popped in a greased pan. For the candy, take one cup of molasses, one cup of light brown or white sugar, one tablespoonful of vinegar. Boil until it will harden in water. Pour on the corn. Stir with a spoon until thoroughly mixed; then mold into balls with the hand.

No flavor should be added to this mixture, as the excellence of this commodity depends entirely upon the united flavor of the corn, salt, and the sugar or molasses.

ENGLISH PLUM PUDDING (THE GENUINE)

from the White House Cookbook, 1894

Soak one pound of stale bread in a pint of hot milk and let it stand and cool. When cold, add to it one-half pound of sugar and the yolks of eight eggs beaten to a cream, one pound of raisins, stoned and floured, one pound of Zante currants, washed and floured, a quarter of a pound of citron cut in slips and dredged with flour, one pound of beef suet, chopped fine and salted, one glass of wine, one glass of brandy, one nutmeg and a tablespoonful of mace, cinnamon and cloves mixed; beat the whole well together and, as the last thing, add the whites of the eight eggs, beaten to a stiff froth; pour into a cloth, previously scalded and dredged with flour, tie it firmly, leaving room for the pudding to swell and boil six hours. Serve with wine or brandy sauce.

It is best to prepare the ingredients the day before and cover closely.

SUET PUDDING, PLAIN
from the White House Cookbook, 1894

One cupful of chopped suet, one cupful of milk, two eggs beaten, half a teaspoonful of salt and enough flour to make a stiff batter, but thin enough to pour from a spoon. Put into a bowl, cover with a cloth, and boil three hours. The same, made a little thinner, with a few raisins added and baked in a well-greased dish is excellent. Two teaspoonfuls of baking powder in the flour improves this pudding. Or if made with sour milk and soda, it is equally as good.

Excerpted from the original
WHITE HOUSE COOKBOOK
1894

---

*M*easures And Weights
In Ordinary Use Among Housekeepers

4 Teaspoonfuls equal 1 tablespoonful liquid.

4 Tablespoonfuls equal 1 wine-glass, or half a gill.

2 Wine-glasses equal one gill or half a cup.

2 Gills equal 1 coffeecupful, or 16 tablespoonfuls.

2 Coffeecupfuls equal 1 pint.

2 Tablespoonfuls equal 1 ounce, liquid.

1 Tablespoonful of salt equals 1 ounce.

16 Ounces equal 1 pound, or a pint of liquid.

4 Coffeecupfuls of sifted flour equal 1 pound.

1 Pint of sugar equals 1 pound. (White granulated.)

2 Coffeecupfuls of powdered sugar equal 1 pound.

1 Coffeecupful of cold butter, pressed down, is one-half pound.

1 Tablespoonful of soft butter, well rounded, equals 1 ounce.

An ordinary tumblerful equals 1 coffeeupful, or half a pint.

About 25 drops of any thin liquid will fill a common sized teaspoon.

1 Pint of finely chopped meat, packed solidly, equals 1 pound.

A set of tin measures (with small spouts or lips), from a gallon down to half a gill, will be found very convenient in every kitchen, though common pitchers, bowls, glasses, etc., may be substituted.

Recipes for Toiletries and Other Household Items.

Cold Cream.

Melt one ounce oil of almonds, half ounce spermaceti, one drachm white wax, and then add two ounces of rose-water, and stir it constantly until cold.

Lip-Salve.

Melt one ounce white wax, one ounce sweet oil, one drachm spermaceti, and throw in a piece of alkanet root to color it, and when cooling, perfume it with oil rose, and then pour it into small white jars or boxes.

For Dandruff.

Take glycerine four ounces, tincture of cantharides five ounces, bay rum four ounces, water two ounces. Mix, and apply once a day and rub well down the scalp.

Hair Invigorator.

Bay rum two pints, alcohol one pint, castor oil one ounce, carb. ammonia half an ounce, tincture of cantharides one ounce. Mix them well. This compound will promote the growth of the hair and prevent it from falling out.

Macassar Oil for the Hair.

Renowned for the past fifty years, is as follows: Take a quarter of an ounce of the chippings of alkanet root, tie this in a bit of coarse muslin and put it in a bottle containing eight ounces of sweet oil; cover it to keep out the dust; let it stand several days; add to this sixty drops of tincture of cantharides, ten drops of oil of rose, neroli and lemon each sixty drops; let it stand one week and you will have one of the most powerful stimulants for the growth of the hair ever known.

Phalon's Instantaneous Hair Dye.

To one ounce of crystallized nitrate of silver, dissolved in one ounce of concentrated aqua ammonia, add one ounce of gum arabic and six ounces of soft water. Keep in the dark. Remember to remove all grease from the hair before applying the dye.

There is danger in some of the patent hair dyes, and hence the *Scientific American* offers what is known as the walnut hair dye. The simplest form is the expressed juice of the bark or shell of green walnuts. To preserve the juice a little alcohol is commonly added to it with a few bruised cloves, and the whole digested together, with occasional agitation, for a week or fortnight, when the clear portion is decanted, and, if necessary, filtered. Sometimes a little common salt is added with the same intention. It should be kept in a cool place. The most convenient way of application is by means of a sponge.

Dye for White or Light Eyebrows.

Boil an ounce of walnut bark in a pint of water for an hour. Add a lump of alum the size of a filbert, and when cold, apply with a camel's-hair brush.

To Remove Freckles.

The following lotion is highly recommended: One ounce of lemon juice, a quarter of a drachm of powdered borax, and half a drachm of sugar; mix in a bottle, and allow them to stand a few days, when the liquor should be rubbed occasionally on the hands and face. Another application is: Friar's balsam one part, rose-water twenty parts.

Powdered nitre moistened with water and applied to the face night and morning, is said to remove freckles without injury to the skin.

Also, a tablespoonful of freshly grated horse-radish, stirred into a cupful of sour milk; let it stand for twelve hours, then strain and apply often. This bleaches the complexion also, and takes off tan.

Cure for Pimples.

One teaspoonful of carbolic acid and one pint of rose-water mixed is an excellent remedy for pimples. Bathe the skin thoroughly and often, but do not let the wash get into the eyes. This wash is soothing to mosquito bites, and irritations of the skin of every nature.

It is advisable, in order to clear the complexion permanently, to cleanse the blood; then the wash would be of advantage.

To obtain a good complexion, a person's diet should receive the first attention. Greasy food, highly spiced soups, hot bread and butter, meats or game, rich gravies, alcoholic liquors, coffee—all are injurious to the complexion. Strong tea used daily will after a time give the skin the color and appearance of leather. Coffee affects the nerves more, but the skin less, and a healthy nervous system is necessary to beauty. Eating between meals, late suppers, over-eating at meals, eating sweetmeats, candies, etc., all these tend to disorder the blood, producing pimples and blotches.

Washing of the face or skin is another consideration for a good complexion; it should be thoroughly washed in plenty of luke-warm water with some mild soap—then rinsed in clear water well; dry with a thick soft towel. If suds are left or wiped off the skin, the action of the air and sun will tan the surface, and permanently deface the complexion; therefore one should be sure to thoroughly rinse off all soap from the skin to avoid the tanning, which will leave a brown or yellow tinge impossible to efface.

For the Sick.

Dishes for invalids should be served in the daintiest and most attractive way; never send more than a supply for one meal; the same dish too frequently set before an invalid often causes a distaste, when perhaps a change would tempt the appetite.

When preparing dishes where milk is used, the condition of the patient should be considered. Long cooking hardens the albumen and makes the milk very constipating; then, if the patient should be already constipated, care should be taken not to heat the milk above the boiling point.

The seasoning of food for the sick should be varied according to the condition of the patient; one recovering from illness can partake of a little piece of roast mutton, chicken, rabbit, game, fish, simply dressed, and simple puddings are all light food and easily digested. A mutton chop, nicely cut, trimmed, and broiled, is a dish that is often inviting to an invalid. As a rule, an invalid will be more likely to enjoy any preparation sent to him if it is served in small delicate pieces. As there are so many small, dainty dishes that can be made for this purpose, it seems useless to try to give more than a small variety of them. Pudding can be made of prepared barley, or tapioca, well soaked before boiling, with an egg added, and a change can be made of light puddings by mixing up some stewed fruit with the puddings before baking; a bread pudding from stale bread crumbs, and a tiny cup-custard, boiled in a small basin or cup; also various drinks, such as milk punch, wine, whey, apple-toddy, and various other nourishing drinks.

Beef Tea.

One pound of lean beef, cut into small pieces. Put into a glass canning jar, without a drop of water, cover tightly and set in a pot of cold water. Heat gradually to a boil and continue this steadily for three or four hours, until the meat is like white rags and juice all drawn out. Season with salt to taste and, when cold, skim.

Veal or Mutton Broth.

Take a scrag-end of mutton (two pounds), put it in a saucepan with two quarts of cold water and an ounce of pearl barley or rice. When it is coming to a boil, skim it well; then add half a teaspoonful of salt; let it boil until half reduced, and then strain it and take off all the fat, and it is ready for use. This is excellent for an invalid. If vegetables are liked in this broth, take one turnip, one carrot, and one onion, cut them in shreds and boil them in the broth half an hour. In that case, the barley may be served with the vegetables in broth.

Oatmeal Gruel.

Put four tablespoonfuls of the best grits (oatmeal coarsely ground) into a pint of boiling water. Let it boil gently, and stir it often, till it becomes as thick as you wish it. Then strain it, and add to it while warm, butter, wine, nutmeg, or whatever is thought proper to flavor it. Salt to taste.

If you make a gruel of fine oatmeal, sift it, mix it first to a thick batter with a little cold water, and then put it into the saucepan of boiling water. Stir it all the time it is boiling, lifting the spoon gently up and down, and letting the gruel fall slowly back again into the pan.

Corn Meal Gruel.

Two tablespoonfuls of fine Indian meal, mixed smooth with cold water, and a saltspoonful of salt; add one quart of boiling water and cook twenty minutes. Stir it frequently, and if it becomes too thick use boiling water to thin it. If the stomach is not too weak, a tablespoonful of cream may be used to cool it. Some like it sweetened and others like it plain. For very sick persons, let it settle, pour off the top, and give without other seasoning. For convalescents, toast a piece of bread as nicely as possible, and put it in the gruel with a tablespoonful of nice sweet cream and a little ginger and sugar. This should be used only when a laxative is allowed.

Slippery-Elm Bark Tea.

Break the bark into bits, pour boiling water over it; cover and let it infuse until cold. Sweeten, ice, and take for summer disorders, or add lemon juice and drink for a bad cold.

Flax-Seed Tea.

Upon one ounce of unbruised flax-seed and a little pulverized liquorice-root pour a pint of boiling (soft or rain) water, and place the vessel containing these ingredients near, but not on, the fire for four hours. Strain through a linen cloth. Make it fresh every day. An excellent drink in fever accompanied by a cough.

Flax-Seed Lemonade.

To a large tablespoonful of flax-seed, allow a tumbler and a half of cold water. Boil them together till the liquid becomes very sticky. Then strain it hot over a quarter-pound of pulverized sugar, and an ounce of pulverized gum arabic. Stir it till quite dissolved, and squeeze into it the juice of a lemon.

This mixture has frequently been found an efficacious remedy for a cold, taking a wine-glass of it as often as the cough is troublesome.

Tamarind Water.

Put tamarinds into a pitcher or tumbler till it is one-third full, then fill up with cold water, cover it, and let it infuse for a quarter of an hour or more. Currant jelly or cranberry juice mixed with water makes a pleasant drink for an invalid.

Arrowroot Wine Jelly.

One cupful of boiling water, one scant tablespoonful of arrowroot, mixed with a little cold water, one tablespoonful of sugar, a pinch of salt, one tablespoonful of brandy, or three tablespoonfuls of wine. Excellent for a sick person without fever.

Soft Toast.

Toast well, but not too brown, two thin slices of stale bread; put them on a warm plate, sprinkle with a pinch of salt, and pour upon them some boiling water; quickly cover with another dish of the same size, and drain off the water. Put a very small bit of butter on the toast and serve at once while hot.

Irish Moss Blanc Mange.

A small handful of moss (to be purchased at any drug store), wash it very carefully, and put it in one quart of milk on the fire. Let the milk simmer for about twenty minutes, or until the moss begins to dissolve. Then remove from the fire and strain through a fine sieve. Add two tablespoonfuls of sugar and half a teaspoonful of vanilla flavoring. Put away to harden in cups or molds, and serve with sugar and cream. A delicate dish for an invalid.

Toast Water, or Crust Coffee.

Take stale pieces of crusts of bread, the end pieces of the loaf, toast them a nice, dark brown, care to be taken that they do not burn in the least, as that affects the flavor. Put the browned crusts into a large milk pitcher, and pour enough boiling water over to cover them; cover the pitcher closely, and let steep until cold. Strain, and sweeten to taste; put a piece of ice in each glass.

This is also good, drunk warm with cream and sugar, similar to coffee.

Plain Milk Toast.

Cut a thin slice from a loaf of stale bread, toast it very quickly, sprinkle a little salt over it, and pour upon it three tablespoonfuls of boiling milk or cream. Crackers split and toasted in this manner, are often very grateful to an invalid.

Linseed Tea.

Put one tablespoonful of linseed into a stewpan with half a pint of cold water; place the stewpan over a moderate fire, and when the water is quite warm, pour it off, and add to the linseed half a pint of fresh cold water, then let the whole boil three or four minutes; season it with lemon and sugar.

Powders for Children.

A very excellent carminative powder for flatulent infants may be kept in the house, and employed with advantage whenever the child is in pain or griped, dropping five grains of oil of anise-seed and two of peppermint on half an ounce of lump sugar, and rubbing it in a mortar, with a drachm of magnesia, into a fine powder. A small quantity of this may be given in a little water at any time, and always with benefit.

For Children Teething.

Tie a quarter of a pound of wheat flour in a thick cloth and boil it in one quart of water for three hours; then remove the cloth and expose the flour to the air or heat until it is hard and dry; grate from it, when wanted, one table-spoonful, which put into half a pint of new milk, and stir over the fire until it comes to a boil, then add a pinch of salt and a tablespoonful of cold water and serve. This gruel is excellent for children afflicted with summer complaint.

Or brown a tablespoonful of flour in the oven or on top of the stove on a baking tin; feed a few pinches at a time to a child and it will often check a diarrhoea. The tincture of "kino"—of which from ten to thirty drops, mixed with a little sugar and water in a spoon, and given every two or three hours, is very efficacious and harmless—can be procured at almost any druggist's. Tablespoon doses of pure cider vinegar and a pinch of salt, has cured when all else failed.

A Bread and Milk Poultice.

Put a tablespoon of the crumbs of stale bread into a gill of milk, and give the whole one boil up. Or, take stale bread crumbs, pour over them boiling water and boil till soft, stirring well; take from the fire and gradually stir in a little glycerine or sweet oil, so as to render the poultice pliable when applied.

Household Hints.

To Destroy Insects and Vermin.

Dissolve two pounds of alum in three or four quarts of water. Let it remain over night till all the alum is dissolved. Then with a brush, apply boiling hot to every joint or crevice in the closet or shelves where croton bugs, ants, cockroaches, etc., intrude; also to the joints and crevices of bedsteads, as bed bugs dislike it as much as croton bugs, roaches, or ants. Brush all the cracks in the floor and mop-boards. Keep it boiling hot while using.

To keep woolens and furs from moths, be sure that none are in the articles when they are put away; then take a piece of strong brown paper, with not a hole through which even a pin can enter. Put the article in it with several lumps of gum camphor between the folds; place this in a close box or trunk. Cover every joint with paper. A piece of cotton cloth, if thick and firm, will answer. Wherever a knitting-needle can pass, the parent moth can enter.

Place pieces of camphor, cedar-wood, Russia leather, tobacco-leaves, whole cloves, or anything strongly aromatic, in the drawers or boxes where furs and other things to be preserved from moths are kept and they will never be harmed. Mice never get into drawers or trunks where gum camphor is placed.

Another Recipe.

Mix half a pint of alcohol, the same quantity of turpentine and two ounces of camphor. Keep in a stone bottle and shake well before using. The clothes or furs are to be wrapped in linen, and crumbled-up pieces of blotting-paper dipped in the liquid to be placed in the box with them, so that it smells strong. This requires renewing but once a year.

Another authority says that a positive, sure recipe is this: Mix equal quantities of pulverized borax, camphor gum and saltpetre together, making a powder. Sprinkle it dry under the edges of carpets, in drawers, trunks, etc.

It will also keep out all kinds of insects, if plentifully used. If the housekeeper will begin at the top of her house with a powder bellows and a large quantity of this fresh powder, and puff it thoroughly into every crack and crevice, whether or not there are croton bugs in them, to the very bottom of her house, special attention being paid to old furniture, closets, and wherever croton water is introduced, she will be freed from these torments. The operation may require repetition, but the end is success.

Moths in Carpets.

If you fear that they are at work at the edge of the carpet, it will sometimes suffice to lay a wet towel, and press a hot flat-iron over it; but the best way is to take the carpet up, and clean it, and give a good deal of attention to the floor. Look in the cracks, and if you discover signs of moths, wash the floor with benzine, and scatter red pepper on it before putting the carpet lining down.

Heavy carpets sometimes do not require taking up every year, unless in constant use. Take out the tacks from these, fold the carpets back, wash the floor in strong suds with a tablespoonful of borax dissolved in it. Dash with insect powder, or lay with tobacco leaves along the edge, and re-tack. Or use turpentine, the enemy of buffalo moths, carpet worms and other insects that injure and destroy carpets. Mix the turpentine with pure water in the proportion of three tablespoonfuls to three quarts of water, and then after the carpet has been well swept, go over each breadth carefully with a sponge dipped in the solution and wrung nearly dry. Change the water as often as it becomes dirty. The carpet will be nicely cleaned as well as disinfected. All moths can be kept away and the eggs destroyed by this means. Spots may be renovated by the use of ox-gall or ammonia and water.

A good way to brighten a carpet is to put half a tumbler of spirits of turpentine in a basin of water, and dip your broom in it and sweep over the carpet once or twice and it will restore the color and brighten it up until you would think it new. Another good way to clean old carpets is to rub them over with meal; just dampen it a very little and rub the carpet with it and when perfectly dry, sweep over with meal. After a carpet is thoroughly swept, rub it with a cloth dipped in water and ammonia; it will brighten the colors and make it look like new.

To Clean Black Lace.

A teaspoonful of gum arabic dissolved in one teacupful of boiling water; when cool, add half a teaspoonful of black ink; dip the lace and spread smoothly between the folds of a newspaper and press dry with book or the like. Lace shawls can be dressed over in this way, by pinning a sheet to the carpet and stretching the shawl upon that; or black lace can be cleaned the same as ribbon and silk. Take an old kid glove (black preferable), no matter how old, and boil it in a pint of water for a short time; then let it cool until the leather can be taken in the hand without burning; use the glove to sponge off the ribbon; if the ribbon is very dirty, dip it into water and draw through the fingers a few times before sponging. After cleaning, lay a piece of paper over the ribbon and iron; paper is better than cloth. The ribbon will look like new.

To Wash White Lace.

First, the soiled laces should be carefully removed from the garment and folded a number of times, keeping the edges evenly together, then based with a coarse thread without a knot in the end. Now put them in a basin of luke-warm suds. After soaking a half hour, rub them carefully between the hands, renewing the suds several times; then, after soaping them well, place them in cold water and let them come to a scald. Take them from this and rinse them thoroughly in luke-warm water, blued a very little, then dip them into a very thin, clear starch, allowing a teaspoonful of starch to a pint of water, so thin that it will be scarcely perceptible. Now roll them in a clean, fresh towel without taking out the bastings; let them lie for an hour or more, iron over several thicknesses of flannel, taking out the bastings of one piece at a time, and ironing on the wrong side, with a moderately hot iron; the laces should be nearly dry, and the points pulled gently with the fingers into shape, before ironing.

To Wash Feathers.

Wash in warm soap-suds and rinse in water a very little blued; if the feather is white, then let the wind dry it. When the curl has come out by washing the feather or getting it damp, place a hot flat-iron so that you can hold the feather just above it while curling. Take a bone or silver knife, and draw the fibres of the feather between the thumb and the dull edge of the knife, taking not more than three fibres at a time, beginning at the point of the feather and curling one-half the other way. The hot iron makes the curl more durable. After a little practice one can make them look as well as new feathers. Or they can be curled by holding them over the stove or range, not near enough to burn; withdraw and shake out; then hold them over again until they curl. When swansdown becomes soiled, it can be washed and look as good as new. Tack strips on a piece of muslin and wash in warm water with white soap, then rinse and hang in the wind to dry. Rip from the muslin and rub carefully between the fingers to soften the feather.

Incombustible Dresses.

By putting an ounce of alum or sal ammoniac in the last water in which muslins or cottons are rinsed, or a similar quantity in the starch in which they are stiffened, they will be rendered almost un-inflammable; or, at least, will with difficulty take the fire, and if they do, will burn without flame. It is astonishing that this simple precaution is so rarely adopted. Remember this and save the lives of your children.

How to Freshen Up Furs.

Furs when taken out in the fall are often found to have a mussed, crushed-out appearance. They can be made to look like new, by following these simple directions: Wet the fur with a hair-brush, brushing up the wrong way of the fur. Leave it to dry in the air for about half an hour, and then give it a good beating on the right side with a rattan. After beating it, comb it with a coarse comb, combing up the right way of the fur.

Facts Worth Knowing.

To Remove the Odor of Onion from fish-kettle and saucepans in which they have been cooked, put wood-ashes or sal soda, potash or lye; fill with water and let it stand on the stove until it boils; then wash in hot suds, and rinse well.

Poison Water—Water boiled in galvanized iron becomes poisonous, and cold water passed through zinc-lined iron pipes should never be used for cooking or drinking. Hot water for cooking should never be taken from hot water pipes; keep a supply heated in kettles.

To Ventilate a Room—Place a pitcher of cold water on a table in your room and it will absorb all the gases with which the room is filled from the respiration of those eating or sleeping in the apartment. Very few realize how important such purification is for the health of the family, or, indeed, understand or realize that there can be any impurity in the rooms; yet in a few hours a pitcher or pail of cold water—the colder the more effective—will make the air of a room pure, but the water will be entirely unfit for use.

To Take Spots from Wash Goods—Rub them with the yolk of an egg before washing.

To Remove Discoloration from Bruises—Apply a cloth wrung out in very hot water, and renew frequently until the pain ceases. Or apply raw beefsteak.

Slicing Pineapples—The knife used for peeling a pineapple should not be used for slicing it, as the rind contains an acid that is apt to cause a swollen mouth and sore lips. The Cubans use salt as an antidote for the ill effects of the peel.

Simple Disinfectant—The following is a refreshing disinfectant for a sick room, or any room that has an unpleasant aroma pervading it: Put some fresh ground coffee in a saucer, and in the centre place a small piece of camphor gum, which light with a match. As the gum burns, allow sufficient coffee to consume with it. The perfume is very pleasant and healthful, being far superior to pastiles, and very much cheaper.

Cure for Hiccough—Sit erect and inflate the lungs fully. Then, retaining the breath, bend forward slowly until the chest meets the knees. After slowly arising again to the erect position, slowly exhale the breath. Repeat this process a second time, and the nerves will be found to have received an access of energy that will enable them to perform their natural functions.

To Keep out Mosquitoes and Rats—If a bottle of the oil of penny-royal is left uncorked in a room at night, not a mosquito, nor any other blood-sucker, will be found there in the morning. Mix potash with powdered meal, and throw it into the rat-holes of a cellar, and the rats will depart. If a rat or a mouse get into your pantry, stuff into its hole a rag saturated with a solution of cayenne pepper, and no rat or mouse will touch the rag for the purpose of opening communication with a depot of supplies.

Choking—A piece of food lodged in the throat may sometimes be pushed down with the finger, or removed with a hair-pin quickly straightened and hooked at the end, or by two or three vigorous blows on the back between the shoulders.

To Prevent Creaking of Bedsteads—If a bedstead creaks at each movement of the sleeper, remove the slats, and wrap the ends of each in old newspapers.

To Banish Rats from the Premises use pounded glass mixed with dry corn meal, placed within their reach. Sprinkling cayenne pepper in their holes will also banish them. Chloride of lime is an infallible remedy, spread around where they come, and thrown into their holes; it should be renewed once in two weeks. Tar is also a a good remedy.

To Prevent the Odor of Boiling Ham or Cabbage—Throw red pepper pods or a few bits of charcoal into the pan they are cooking in.

INDEX

MORE HEALTHY TITLES

❏ **Magic Beans,** *Patti Bazel Geil, M.S., R.D., C.D.E.*—Beans are proven to help reduce the risk of obesity and illness including heart disease, diabetes, and cancer. This collection of 150 recipes maximizes the health benefits while offering creative and sumptuous dishes even the toughest bean skeptics will enjoy, with preparation and cooking taking only minutes.

0776   ISBN: 0-471-34747-7 $12.95

❏ **Skim the Fat,** *The American Dietetic Association*—From the world's foremost experts on nutrition comes the definitive guide for reducing the fat in everything we eat. *Skim the Fat* will show you how to reduce your fat intake to lower your risk for heart disease, cancer, stroke, and a myriad of other diseases—while helping you lose weight.

0628   ISBN: 0-471-34703-5 $10.95

❏ **366 Low-Fat Brand-Name Recipes in Minutes,** *M.J. Smith, R.D.*—Here's more than a year's worth of the fastest family favorites using the country's most popular brand-name foods—from Minute Rice to Ore Ida—while reducing unwanted calories, fat, salt, and cholesterol.

0504   ISBN: 0-471-34654-3 $12.95

❏ **All-American Low-Fat Meals in Minutes,** *M.J. Smith, R.D.*—Filled with tantalizing recipes and valuable tips, this cookbook makes great-tasting low-fat foods a snap for holidays, special occasions, or everyday. Most recipes take only minutes to prepare.

1735   ISBN: 0-471-34655-1 $14.95

❏ **60 Days of Low-Fat, Low-Cost Meals in Minutes,** *M.J. Smith, R.D.,* More than 150 quick and sumptuous recipes complete with the latest nutrition facts for lowering calories, fat, salt, and cholesterol. This book contains complete menus for 60 days and recipes that use ingredients found in virtually grocery store—for a total cost of less than $10.

0105   ISBN: 0-471-34652-7 $12.95

❏ **One Year of Healthy, Hearty & Simple One-Dish Meals,** *Pam Spaude and Jan Owan-McMenamin, R.D.*—This collection is packed with easy-to-make, healthy, and tasty family favorites and unique creations that are meals in themselves—and most take under 30 minutes to prepare.

0199   ISBN: 0-471-34691-8 $14.95